Hikes around the Columbia Valley

Stefanie Mclellan and Corinna Strauss

DEDICATION

To my favorite hiking partners: Cam, Anna, and Henry - *SM*

For my love of the natural world and my beloved hiking partner, Ila Bean - *CS*

CONTENTS

DISCLAIMER

Hiking and scrambling are not without risks. There is a possibility of wildlife encounters, hazardous weather conditions, getting lost, rockfall, river crossings, and many more risks. Trails and scrambles described in this book may change. Roads may become deactivated and new roads may be built. There is also risk to driving on backroads - you may run into logging trucks or washed out bridges. You may have car trouble many kilometers from a paved road. By providing you with the information in this book we are in no way responsible for any injuries or property damage you might sustain. **You as the guidebook user are entirely responsible for managing your own risk when traveling into the mountains.** If you lack knowledge and experience, hire a guide or go with a more experienced friend. Learn as much as you can and leave a plan with someone. Be prepared. There is also a significant risk to staying on your couch and eating junk food. You may die of a heart attack or suffer from depression. When weighing the risks of traveling into the mountains versus the risks of staying on the couch, we know which we would choose.

ACKNOWLEDGMENT

The original Hikes around Invermere by Aaron Cameron and Matt Gunn has been a trusted companion for years. The authors clearly researched their book well. The photos of using a trail wheel in the era when GPS devices were still in their infancy speak to the level of commitment that was required to write the book. However, many things have changed in the quarter century since the book was written. Some trails are no longer accessible as they now cross private land. Many access roads have changed. Some trails have become overgrown while new trails have been established. It was time to write an updated guidebook!

We would like to acknowledge that there were people living in these mountains and valleys long before the arrival of European explorers and settlers. There is rich local indigenous history dating back thousands of years. Many of the peaks, rivers, and lakes have indigenous names, and many trails were first established by indigenous travelers. We would like to recognize that we are grateful to live and recreate on the unceded traditional and ancestral territory of the Ktunaxa and Secwepemc First Nations.

We would also like to thank the trail builders. They are the ones who quietly build and maintain the trails that we all enjoy. The Summit Trailmakers Society in Invermere is responsible for a number of trails. Support them - buy a membership or help out with a trail maintenance party. There are many other unsung heroes who build and maintain trails. Buy them a beer. Many guide outfitters also help maintain trails. Thank them by treating their property with respect.

We would like to thank the many people who contributed to this book – especially those who shared their photos and knowledge. We feel fortunate to be part of this wonderful community of mountain people.

We hope that you will discover many wonderful places to hike in these pages. We are fortunate to have such a large, wild area to call home. Please leave no trace and use social media responsibly.

Happy trails!

Stefanie Mclellan and Corinna Strauss

INTRODUCTION

HIKING SEASON

Some of the valley trails can be used year round. Several trails, such as the Johnson and the Nipika trails, are used in the winter by nordic skiers and fat bikers. Trails such as the Spirit Trail or Mount Swansea melt out by April while trails in the high alpine are usually not accessible until July. Flowers will be at their peak in July and August. Most years the hiking season extends well into October. Larch season - mid September to early October - is a magical time for hiking.

Larch Madness. Photo: AJ McGrath

WILDLIFE

The Columbia Valley is an exceptional place to be. We share this landscape with many different types of wildlife. Remember this is their home just as much as ours. With all wildlife, please keep your distance, never feed or interfere with wildlife and keep your pets under control. Bear safety and awareness is one of the most important factors when out hiking and in the backcountry. Please always be bear aware, carry bear spray, know how to use it and take the proper precautions to avoid bear encounters. Here are the main key points of avoiding a bear encounter.

- Make noise with your voice
- Travel in groups when possible
- Watch for signs of bears such as, fresh scat, diggings and carcasses (fresh kills)
- Carry bear spray that is readily available, and know how to use it.

If you have a bear encounter or an encounter with dangerous wildlife, please report it to the Conservation Service RAPP (Report All Poachers & Polluters) 1 877-952-7277.

WildSafeBC offers free online courses in wildlife, bear safety and the proper use of bear spray. Please see the link to access the courses and the WildSafeBC website.

https://wildsafebc.com/learn/courses-and-training/

BACKROADS DRIVING

Most of the trails in this book are accessed via logging roads. Driving on these roads is very different from driving on a highway. For one, they are built primarily for logging trucks and these trucks always have the right of way. Give them much more room than you think they need. It is best to carry a radio and call in your position to avoid any conflicts.

The state of these roads changes frequently as some become deactivated while new roads get built so if in doubt inquire with the local timber companies regarding the current status of the roads. Getting a Backroads Mapbook is useful though the maps may not always be current.

Photo: Rob Orchiston, Toby Creek December 2020

Make sure your vehicle is in good shape. Getting a vehicle towed out of the bush costs thousands of dollars and is not covered by roadside insurance. Carry a spare tire, jumper cables, and basic tools. A portable compressor/battery charger may be worth having in your vehicle in case your battery is dead or your tire flat at a remote trailhead. Have a communication device in case you run into trouble. Carry a saw in case there are trees across the road. A shovel and piece of rope could also be useful. Wrapping your vehicle with chicken wire is a good idea in some places to prevent porcupines from chewing your brake lines or tires while you are out hiking. Some areas such as the Bugaboos are notorious for this, however some people do not take any chances and always wrap their vehicle.

What kind of vehicle you need depends on your comfort level to some degree: some people may be very comfortable beating up their old Honda Civic while bashing into the Bugaboos while others would not dream of driving their new SUV on any gravel roads. In general, for most trails accessed by logging roads a small SUV or a Subaru type vehicle with all wheel drive and slightly higher clearance is sufficient. In a few places you will require 4x4 and high clearance to access the trailhead. This will be mentioned in the description. If your car is not up to the task, consider bringing a mountain bike to carry you the last few kilometers.

Photo: Pat Morrow

SAFETY

The widespread availability of satellite communication devices has led to an increase in the number of people heading into the mountains without being properly prepared. It is now possible to call for a rescue at the push of a button. However, simply being tired, running out of food, or having minor injuries are poor reasons to launch a rescue. Not only does it cost taxpayer money but it requires Search and Rescue volunteers to leave their homes and potentially put themselves at risk to come save you. Be self sufficient and well prepared.

1. Plan Ahead
Research the route by reading maps, guidebooks, and websites. Think about your skills and fitness level. What is the weather forecast? What gear will you need? Is the route in condition? Assess your experience. If you are unsure of your skills, take a course, hire a guide, or go with a more experienced friend.

2. Take a Wilderness First Aid course
Know what to do for minor injuries and know when you need a rescue. There is a list of recommended providers in the back.

3. Bring the 10 Essentials (and more)

10 ESSENTIALS	
Navigation	Map, compass, GPS
Sun Protection	Hat, sunscreen, long sleeved shirt
Extra Clothing	Rain gear, warm layers
Headlamp	And spare batteries
First Aid Kit	Appropriate for trip length and group size
Fire Starter	Waterproof matches, lighter
Repair Kit	Multitool, duct tape etc.
Food and Water	plus water treatment tablets and extra food
Signaling Device	Mirror, whistle
Emergency Shelter	Space blanket, bivy bag, or tarp

4. Leave a Trip Plan
You can use the Adventure Smart app to send a trip plan to a friend. Or else, leave a detailed written plan describing your route, equipment, and when you should be back by. Don't forget to check back in.

5. Be Prepared to Turn Around
Re-evaluate the weather, conditions, and your group's energy level

throughout the day and always be prepared to turn around if things change.

6. Carry a Communication Device

Most locations in this book have no cell service. A satellite messaging device, such as an InReach or Spot is essential, whether for vehicle trouble, to check in, or to tell your loved ones you will be back later than anticipated. In an emergency they can be used to call for a rescue.

Check out https://www.adventuresmart.ca/ for more information.

Bugaboos

SCRAMBLING

Scrambling generally involves climbing mountains without the use of ropes. It is usually more difficult than hiking on a trail but less technical than roped climbing. However, it does not necessarily mean it is safer than roped climbing. Scrambling safely depends to a large degree on the ability to read terrain and to find the easiest, and safest route. This is a skill which requires experience and good judgment. If you lack experience, take a scrambling course or go with an experienced friend. Start on easy objectives with minimal exposure and hazards, and build experience.

Rockfall is a real possibility on many scrambling routes. Wear a helmet and be very mindful not to kick rocks onto those below you. Falling - either because of a hold breaking loose, or losing your footing on slippery rocks or snow - is always a concern. Maintain 3 points of contact and test holds before committing your weight to them.

If you will travel on snow, consider bringing an ice axe and crampons, or microspikes for lower angle terrain, and learn how to self-arrest if you should fall. Snow slopes may pose an avalanche risk, especially in spring and early summer. Cornices can be very dangerous. They are prone to collapse without warning. It can be hard to tell from above if you are on solid ground or cornice and it is important to probe and give them a wide berth. It is also dangerous to travel below cornices, especially if they are baking in the heat.

Descending from a climb is usually harder than ascending therefore if you feel you are at your limits climbing up consider turning around as it will likely be more difficult coming down. Being prepared to turn around at any point - whether due to fatigue, weather, conditions, or the degree of difficulty encountered - is very important in staying safe. It is also important to know when a route might not be in shape. A route that could be easy scrambling when the rock is dry could be very difficult when covered in snow. Lichen covered rocks become extremely slippery when wet. A thin veneer of ice on rocks (called verglas) can make rocks extremely slippery and scrambling could be dangerous.

We have given scrambles the following ratings:

Easy:
Mostly off trail hiking, with minimal route finding and exposure.
Example: Mount Brewer

Moderate:
More hands on climbing, some route finding, mild exposure.
Example: Mount Aeneas

Difficult:
Significant route finding, exposure, hands on climbing, and rockfall risk.
Example: Mount Nelson

WEATHER

Mountain weather can change quickly. It can snow any time of year. It is not uncommon to be in a snowstorm in the high mountains in August while it is 30 degrees in the valley. Lightning storms are a concern, especially when traveling above tree line. Check the latest weather forecast before heading out.

These are useful weather resources:

- The Panorama Alpine Weather forecast is available year-round and especially useful for the Toby Creek/Panorama/Brewer area: https://www.panoramaresort.com/panorama-today/daily-snow-report/
- SpotWx is a free online weather program which provides computer weather modelling for any location: https://spotwx.com/
- Avalanche Canada produces a year-round big picture mountain weather forecast: https://www.avalanche.ca/weather/forecast

NAVIGATION

Map and compass are the traditional method of navigating however they require training and practice. Most topographical maps in Canada have not been updated since the 1970s and therefore are of limited utility as they often do not show newer trails, logging roads or other features. Many people now use their cell phones for navigation. However, battery life is a concern, especially in cold temperatures. Bring a back-up navigation method and back-up batteries for devices. A handheld GPS can also be helpful as the batteries often last much longer than a phone's battery. These devices need to have maps loaded onto them before use.

The following smartphone apps are useful for backcountry travel:

- AllTrails (requires subscription for offline use)
- Gaia (requires subscription)
- Topo Canada (free)
- TrailForks (the free version allows user to download one area)
- Google Maps. You can download the desired area for offline use beforehand. This is especially useful for satellite images as they show logging roads and cut blocks not shown on maps.
- Avenza is a platform which allows users to download maps from a map store, many of which are free. It integrates those maps with the phone's GPS function. The Backroads Mapbook is available on Avenza which can be helpful for backroad driving.

HOW TO USE THIS BOOK

The book has been divided into geographic sections by drainage or access road. It starts with hikes in the valley, many of which are easy walks, often accessible year-round and great for family or after work hikes. The next part of the book covers the Purcells, from south to north. The last part covers the Rockies, from north to south. The book generally covers an area from Spillimacheen to Premier lake. Both hiking times and distances have been given. The hiking times are approximate, and for a reasonably fit person. Times and distances are usually round trip, except where indicated. Be aware that logging roads change frequently and that the access description in this book may be different from the time of writing.

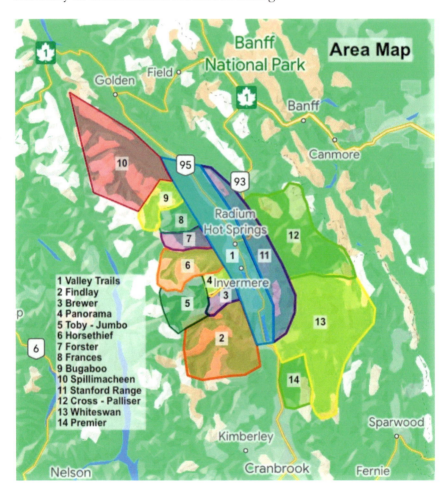

THE CLASSICS

While we think all the hikes described in this book have merit, there are some that are just above and beyond. If you want great scenery, flowers, lakes and vistas - start with these trails. However, they tend to be popular. Do not expect solitude. They are listed in no particular order. You will notice that some day hikes also make great backpacking trips.

Day Hikes:
- Diana Lake
- Mount Pinto
- Pedley Pass
- Brewer Tarns
- Jumbo Pass
- Mount Bruce
- Lake of the Hanging Glaciers
- Welsh Lakes
- Buster (Azure) Lake
- Kain Hut/Applebee Dome

Limestone Lakes

Backpacking Trips:
- Limestone Lakes
- Diana Lake
- Ben Abel Lakes
- Earl Grey Pass
- Jumbo Pass
- Lake of the Hanging Glaciers
- Welsh Lakes
- Kain Hut/Applebee Dome

Hikes at a glance

Hike		Total Distance	Total Time	Elevation gain	Good for:
Valley Hikes					
1	**Hoodoos**	2.5 km	45 min	120 m	Kids, shoulder season, *interesting geological* formation
2	**Westside Legacy Trail**	50 km	varies	680m	Paved trail. Mainly used by cyclists. Many shorter options.
3	**SRL (Salter Creek)**	8.4 km	2 hours	330 m	Lake views, dogs, shoulder season, mountain biking, trail running
4	**Windermere Lake Park**	9 km	2 - 3 hours	240 m	Flowers, shoulder season
5	**Spirit Trail**	18.4 km	4-5 hours	90 m	Early season, lake views. Shorter options.
6	**Wilmer Wetlands**	5 km	1-2 hours	138 m	Birdwatching
7	**Lake Enid**	2 km	30 min	20 m	Birdwatching, swimming, kids
8	**Old Coach and Deja Vu**	15.4 km	4 hours	413 m	Shoulder season, wetland views
9	**Juniper-Sinclair**	7.7 km	2 hours	281 m	Waterfall, shoulder season, canyon views
10	**The Kloosifier**	7.6 km	2 hours	240 m	Canyon views, shoulder season, biking, trail running
11	**The Johnson**	9.5 km	2-3 hours	378 m	Canyon views, shoulder season, biking, trail running
12	**Valley Trail**	4 km	1.5 hours	160 m	Paved trail, shoulder season, creek
13	**Fairmont Trails**	varies	Few hours	varies	Short trails around Fairmont Hot Springs
14	**Lower Bugaboo Falls**	2.9 km	2 hours	135 m	Easy hike to a nice waterfall, good for kids
15	**Marion Benchlands**	11.5km	2-3 hours	285 m	Shoulder season, birdwatching

Hike		Total Distance	Total Time	Elevation gain	Good for:
Findlay Creek					
16	**Doctor Creek**	12-14km	3-4 hours	500-600m	Larches, off trail exploring, mining relics
17	**Findlay Creek to Morigeau Basin**	66km	multi day	900m	Wilderness adventure, mountaineering
Brewer Creek					
18	**Brewer Tarns**	10 km	3 hours	450 m	Easy access to subalpine meadows and tarns, good for kids
19	**Mount Brewer**	12.9 km	4-5 hours	959 m	Easy scramble, great views
20	**Ben Abel Lake**	28 km	2 days	1000m/1150m	Stunning hike to a beautiful lake with nice camping and good fishing
Panorama					
21	**Mount Goldie***	14 km	6-8 hours	1100 m	Easy scramble, Great views, lift option
22	**Goldie Lake***	15.5 km	6-8 hours	895 m	Beautiful tarn, lift option, larches
23	**Goldie Plateau via Taynton Creek**	18 km	5-7 hours	1300 m	Larches, great views
24	**Panorama to Brewer***	15.4 km one way	multi day	1095 m	Interesting subalpine hike to connect two areas, lift option
25	**Hopeful Ridge (Cannery)**	25 km	8-10 hours	1590 m	Great views, alpine ridge hike
26	**Castle Rock Trail**	8.5 km	3-4 hours	690 m	Steep trail to prominent view point

*add 7.4 km total distance and 426 m elevation if not taking Mile 1 Lift

Hike		Total Distance	Total Time	Elevation gain	Good for:
Toby Creek - Jumbo Creek					
27	**Mount Nelson**	10.4 km	8-10 hours	1897m	Difficult scramble to prominent peak
28	**Delphine Glacier**	24 km	1-2 days	1510 m	Bike-hike combo Glacier views, off trail route
29	**Thunderbird Mine**	15.6 km	5-6 hours	970m	Old mine site Alpine basin
30	**Earl Grey Pass**	36 km	2 days	1315m	Backpacking, glacier views, flowers. Option to continue to West Kootenays
31	**Black Diamond Basin**	16 km	4-6 hours	1025m	Alpine basin, flowers, fall colors
32	**Jumbo Pass**	8 km	3-4 hours	712 m	Flowers, views, cabin, camping
33	**Bastille Mountain**	4 km	2-3 hours	300 m	Moderate scramble from Jumbo Pass, great views
Horsethief Creek					
34	**Mount Bruce**	6.4 km	3 hours	664 m	Flowers, views, larches
35	**Redline Peak**	14 km	5-7 hours	1200 m	Moderate scrambling
36	**Commander Glacier**	4.5 km	2-3hours	350 m	Glacier views
37	**Farnham Glacier**	8 km	3-4 hours	220 m	Summer skiing, glacier views, cabin
38	**Lake of the Hanging Glaciers**	16 km	6-8 hours	947 m	Glacier views, lake
39	**Glacier Dome Subpeak**	4 km	3 hours	400 m	Moderate scramble from Lake of the Hanging Glacier
Forster Creek					
40	**Irish Lakes**	12 km	4-5 hours	830 m	Waterfalls, larches, alpine lake
41	**Welsh Lakes**	8+ km	3-4 hours	550 m	Lakes, flowers, larches, camping

Hike		Total Distance	Total Time	Elevation gain	Good for:
Forster Creek					
42	**Olive Hut/ Catamount Glacier**	15 km	5-7 hours	945 m	Glacier travel Alpine cabin
43	**Thunderwater Lake**	14 km	5-7 hours	455 m	Lake views, camping, off trail hiking
Frances Creek					
44	**Azure Lake/ Buster Lake**	10.5 km	4-5 hours	767 m	Lake views, option to connect to Mclean via high traverse
45	**McLean Lake**	11.4 km	3-4 hours	575 m	Lake views, option to connect to Buster/Azure via high traverse
46	**Septet Pass**	19 km	5-7 hours	620 m	Alpine meadows
47	**Shangri La via Tiger Pass**	12 km	4-5 hours	1200 m	Pocket glacier crossing, alpine, wildflowers, lakes, camping
48	**Mount Ethelbert**	3 km (from Shangri La)	3-4 hours	960 m	Moderate scramble from Shangri la
Bugaboo Creek					
49	**Templeton Lake**	9.4 km	4 hours	280 m	Waterfall, lake, option to connect to Shangri La
50	**Rockypoint Creek**	17 km	6-7 hours	1050m	Camping, views, alpine meadow
51	**Cobalt Lake**	15.1 km	5-7 hours	1216 m	Lake, views, camping
52	**Conrad Kain Hut/Applebee**	10 km	3-5 hours	991 m	Mountain views, glaciers, flowers, cabin, camping
53	**Eastpost Spire**	3 km (from Applebee)	3-4 hours	530 m	Difficult scramble from Applebee, great views
54	**Silver Basin**	6 km	3 hours	500m	Alpine meadows, views of the Bugaboos
55	**Chalice Ridge**	15.6 km	5-6 hours	1000 m	Wildflowers, views of the bugaboos, off trail hiking
56	**Bugaboo Pass**	10 km	3-4 hours	660m	Views, glaciers, flowers

Hike		Total Distance	Total Time	Elevation gain	Good for:
Spillimacheen Valley					
57	**Hobo Ridge**	12.5 km +	3-4 hours	650 m	views, alpine meadows
58	**Silent Pass**	4 km	1-2 hours	360 m	Beautiful subalpine area with great views of the Selkirks
59	**International Basin**	20 km	Multi day	1500m	Route finding, glacier travel, cabin, flowers, alpine scenery
60	**Bald Hills**	25+ km	2-3 days	500m	Extensive alpine meadows with glacier views, lodge, camping
61	**Copperstain Mountain**	8.5 km (from Yurt Hollow)	3-4 h	700m	Easy scramble, views, access from Bald Hills hike
Stanford Range					
62	**Diana Lake**	14 km	3-4 hours	780 m	fishing, teahouse, larches, flowers
63	**The Judge**	6 km (from Diana Lake)	3 h (from Diana Lake)	589m	easy scramble
65	**Kimpton Creek**	10.1 km	2-3 hours	508 m	Short hike in the forest, shoulder season, rainy days
64	**Redstreak Creek**	4.5 km	1-2 hours	204 m	Short hike in the forest, shoulder season, rainy days
66	**Kindersley-Sinclair**	16 km	4-5 hours	1341 m	Wildflowers, views. Minimum group size due to bear activity
67	**Cobb Lake**	5 km	2-3 hours	246 m	Good for kids, fishing, snowshoeing
68	**Dog Lake**	5.1 km	2-3 hours	333 m	Good for kids. Can also be biked or snowshoed
69	**Redstreak Mountain**	16 km	5-7hours	1610m	Difficult scramble, great views
70	**Mount Swansea loop**	12 km	3-4 h	750 m	Views, early season
71	**Four Point Mountain**	6.7 km	3 hours	937 m	Views, early season

Hike		Total Distance	Total Time	Elevation gain	Good for:
Stanford Range					
72	**Mount Pinto**	8.7 km	3-4 hours	960 m	Great views, easy scramble
73	**Mount Bryan**	6.5kms	4 hours	950 m	No trail, route finding skills needed, a great local adventure.
74	**Pedley Pass**	10.5 km	3-4 hours	677 m	Flowers, scenery
75	**Mount Aeneas**	8.6 km	4-5 hours	834 m	Moderate scramble from Pedley Pass - views
76	**Chisel Peak**	10 km	6-8 hours	1300 m	Moderate scramble
77	**Mount Tegart**	7.2 km	2-3 hours	930 m	Easy scramble
78	**Fairmont Mountain**	3 km	2 hours	500 m	Moderate scramble
Cross River/Palliser River					
79	**Nipika - Natural Bridge**	11 km - many options	3 h	332 m	Hiking, running, cross-country skiing, biking, fat biking, dogs. Trail fees in winter.
80	**Mitchell Ridge**	10.5 km	4-5 hours	995 m	Ridgeline hike, great views, option to continue along ridge
81	**Assiniboine Lake**	14 km	4-5 hours	665 m	Lakes, mountain views, option to access Mt Assiniboine via glacier
82	**Marvel Pass**	14 km	4-5 hours	760 m	Views, flowers
83	**Marvel Peak/Penny's Peak**	17.2 km	5-7 hours	1007 m	Easy scramble Views
84	**Whiteman Pass**	10 km	3-4 hours	689 m	Short hike to subalpine meadows, options for scrambling and exploring
85	**Ralph Lake**	9 km	3-4 hours	902 m	Alpine lake, fishing, scrambling, larches, flowers, camping
86	**Queen Mary Lake**	20.5km	Multi day	995 m	alpine lake, camping, cabin, scrambling, fishing
87	**Limestone Lakes**	35.2 km	Multi day	2018 m	Camping, interesting karst topography, beautiful lakes, off trail hiking

Hike		Total Distance	Total Time	Elevation gain	Good for:
Whiteswan and Beyond					
88	**Gibraltar Lookout**	8.5 km	3-4 hours	785 m	Views, old fire lookout
89	**Whiteswan Ridge**	8.5 km	4-5 hours	910 m	Ridgewalk, easy scramble, views
90	**Whiteswan Northshore**	10-20km	3-6 hours	200 m	Rainy days, lake views, camping
91	**Ptarmigan Lake**	12 km	3-4 hours	700 m	Lake views, fishing
92	**White Knight Peak**	5 km	3-4 hours	800 m	Moderate scramble from Ptarmigan lake
93	**Graves Lookout**	11.6 km	4-5 hours	883 m	Flowers, views ruins of an old fire lookout
94	**Russell Lake**	15 km	1-2 days	505m	Beautiful alpine lake
95	**Fish Lake**	12.6 km	4-5 hours	495m	Cabin, lake, camping, biking, great for kids
96	**Sparkle Lake**	5.6km	1-2 hours	360m	Views
97	**Wildhorse Ridge**	6.4km	2-3hours	640m	Views, flowers
98	**Alpine Viewpoint**	6.4km	2-3 hours	600m	Views of alpine plateau
99	**Summer Pass**	8 km	3-4 hours	430m	Views, alpine, flowers
100	**Sugarloaf**	14 km	5-6 hours	368m	Views
101	**Connor Lakes**	14.4 km	5-6 hours	480 m	Lakes, fishing, cabin
Premier Lake					
102	**Shark Tooth**	12km	4-5 hours	900m	Wildflowers, cool limestone formations, near warm springs
103	**Saddleback Ridge**	12 km	7-8 hours	1134 m	Steep trail with great views
104	**Yankee Canuck Turtle**	6.2km	2 hours	250m	Early season, good for kids
105	**Premier Ridge**	8km	2-3 hours	300m	Early season flowers, off trail hiking

VALLEY TRAILS

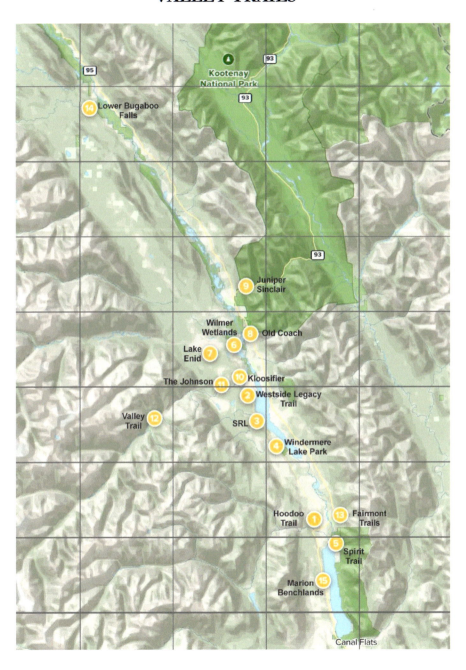

1 Hoodoo Trail

Distance 2.5 km
Time 45 min
Elevation Gain 120 m
Map Page 29

Hoodoos in winter

The Hoodoo trail is a short scenic trail which leads to the top of the prominent rock formations along the highway just west of Fairmont.

Access:
From Fairmont drive south on highway 93/95. After 3.3 km turn right on Westside Road. After 1.2km turn left into the parking lot.

Trail:
The Hoodoo trail is on land owned by the Nature Trust and the Nature Conservancy of Canada. In 2017 a loop trail was built to make access to the top of the Hoodoos safer and to protect the environmentally and culturally sensitive area around the Hoodoos. From the parking lot head uphill through the forest reaching the loop trail after 1 km. Several interpretive signs describe the ecological and cultural history of the area. From the top enjoy panoramic views of the Columbia Valley. Look for several species of bird such as white throated swifts and violet green swallows.

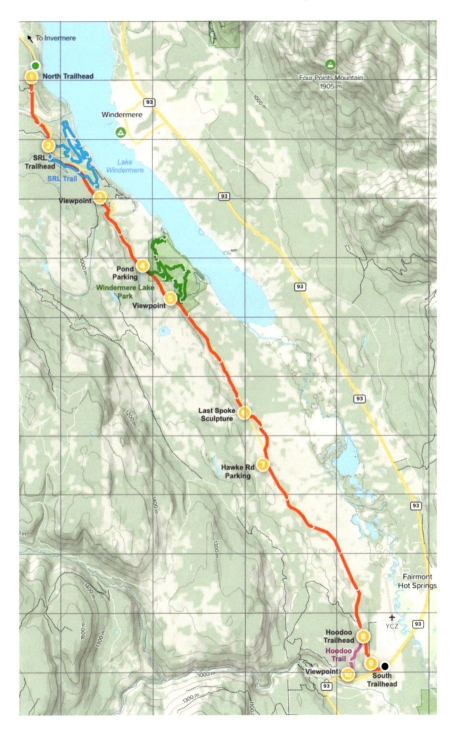

2 Markin -MacPhail Westside Legacy Trail

Distance 25 km one way
Time varies
Elevation Gain 300 m one way

This 25 km paved trail connecting Invermere to Fairmont was completed in 2020. While it is popular with cyclists, it also has pleasant sections for walking and is a good early season option. Expect cyclists to be traveling fast and watch for them, especially on blind corners. Cyclists should yield to walkers however they may not always expect them. The trail is fully wheelchair/stroller accessible. Each trailhead has an outhouse, a picnic table and a bike tool station and there are several benches and picnic tables along the way.

The trail has some hilly sections, especially at the north end. An out and back of the entire trail is 50 km with about 600 m elevation gain in total.

Access:
The northern trailhead is located 3.6 km south of Invermere on Westside Road. The southern trailhead is located just west of Fairmont. From Fairmont, take Hwy 93 south. After 3.3 km turn right onto Westside Road. The trailhead is located on the right after 300 m metres.

Recommended sections for hiking:

Salter Creek to Brady Creek – 6 km roundtrip
Park at the SRL parking lot which is located 4.8 km south of Invermere on the right, or 2.3 km south of the northern trailhead. Walk south, crossing Salter Creek before gradually gaining elevation through open forest. As you gain elevation you get great views of Lake Windermere. Continue all the way to Brady Creek before returning the same way.

Westside Legacy Trail - Salter Creek to Brady Creek Section

Hawke Road to K2 hill – 12 km roundtrip

From Invermere drive south on Westside Road for 16.4 km and park at Hawke Road on the right. From Fairmont drive north on Westside Road for 7.4 km and turn left. Cross the road and start walking north on the trail. It soon veers away from the road into a pleasant little valley. After a kilometer it crosses the road again, passing the Last Spoke sculpture. Continue along the trail, parallel to the road but set back a little. This section is shady and flat. Eventually the trail crosses the entrance to the K2 ranch. Here start switchbacking up the hill. At the height of land there is a picnic table. Enjoy views of the Fairmont range and return the way you came.

Beaver Pond Loop – 2.5 km loop

This is the newest section of trail. Park at the pond 11 km south of Invermere. Start by going north on the trail. After a few hundred meters you will come to a junction. Go left, to go clockwise around a beaver pond and eventually reach Westside Road. Walk along the road for 200 meters before getting back on the trail to loop back to the start.

3 SRL (Salter Creek)

Distance: 8.4 km
Time: 2 hours
Elevation Gain: 330 m

This is a scenic trail close to town. It goes through grasslands and open forest with views of Lake Windermere. It is located on private land. The landowners graciously allow hiking and biking. Please treat the land with respect.

Looking across Lake Windermere on the SRL trail

Access:
From Invermere drive south on Westside Road for 4.8 km. Park in the parking lot on the right.

Trail:
The trail starts across from the parking area on the other side of Westside road. It winds through the trees for a few hundred meters before turning right on an old road bed. It then goes downhill through the trees, briefly coming within view of the road. You slowly lose elevation as the trail contours along a dry hillside before leveling out. When it reaches a flat section, continue right on the trail. It continues to drop through the trees.

Here you will get the first of many nice views of the lake. The trail now climbs up again before dropping down through some open grasslands. Eventually you reach a shady section where it follows an old road bed again. Cross the creek on some slippery logs before climbing out of the ravine. At the top of the hill are some stunning views of Lake Windermere. The trail winds along through the trees before it reaches Westside Road. Turn left and follow the road for 100 m. Cross over by the large gate leading into the SRL property. The trail continues just left of the gate. It now climbs steadily. At the height of land it crosses the Westside Legacy Trail (watch for cyclists) and continues through the forest before reaching the paved trail again. Here you can follow the pavement back to the parking lot. If you would rather continue on single track, follow the paved trail until you reach a short gravel road going uphill just past some S bends in the paved trail. Go uphill until the fence and then rejoin the single track which comes out just before Salter Creek. Follow the paved trail back to the parking lot for a few hundred meters.

4 Windermere Lake Provincial Park

Distance: 9 km
Time: 2 - 3 hours
Elevation Gain: 240 m

This small provincial park has several unmarked trails, some of which go right to the lakeshore. It is a peaceful walk through open grasslands and forests. Bank swallows nest in the cliffs near the shore.

Access:

From Invermere drive south for 11 km on Westside road and park at the pond. Follow the road for a couple hundred meters then look for a gate and a fence on the left side. A wooden post marks the park.

Trail:

Follow the fairly obvious trail as it drops in elevation, reaching open grasslands. At the bottom you reach the train tracks just before the shoreline. Return the way you came but when you reach the forest again look for a faint trail to the left. Follow this trail for a few hundred meters and eventually it turns left and downhill again. The trail is fairly indistinct in spots but continue down and slightly trending right. Eventually it leads over some steep dirt whoops and then starts climbing uphill again. Before the fence line the trail goes right, through the forest. Eventually you regain the trail you started on. After 300 m look for a faint trail to the left. This trail gains elevation and eventually reaches a view point before turning right again and going downhill through the forest, leading back to the start.

5 Spirit Trail

Distance: up to 18.4 km
Time: 4-5 hours
Elevation Gain: 90 m

This 16 km loop trail meanders through pine forest and meadows on the east shore of Columbia Lake, occasionally going along the shore line. It is often one of the first trails that is snow free in spring. It has beautiful views of Columbia Lake and the Purcells to the west. Expect to share the trail with mountain bikers.

Access:
From Fairmont Hot Springs head south on the highway. As you go down the hill turn left by the fire hall onto Fairmont Creek Road. Take the next right onto Columbia River Road. This eventually turns into a gravel road. Drive all the way to the end, about 1.6 km.

Spirit Trail and Columbia Lake

Trail:
From the parking area head west on a well built trail. After 300 metres you reach the shore of Columbia Lake. The trail now turns south, paralleling the shore line and meandering through the woods. Eventually it turns east again

as a small inlet blocks the way. To hike the full length of the Spirit trail turn right at a 4 way junction. Where the trail breaks into the open cross a dirt track and continue along the trail as it makes a loop, eventually reaching the same spot. Backtrack a short section to the four way intersection and this time taking the right. The trail now climbs slightly through open forest before breaking out into open grasslands again. After 3 km take a trail to the left, shortly after you cross a little ravine and head downhill back to the parking lot.

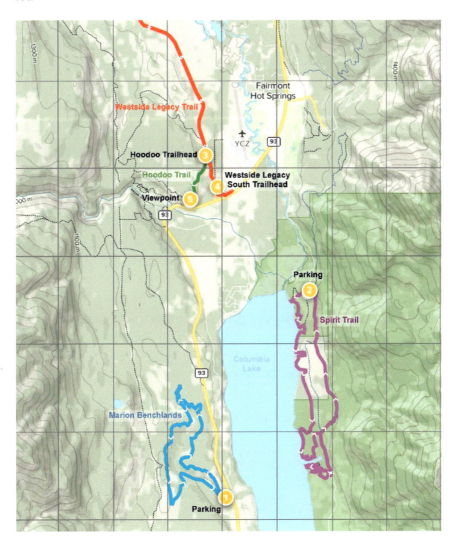

6 Wilmer Wetlands

Distance: 5 km
Time: 1-2 hours
Elevation Gain: 138 m

A short hike along cliffs to the wetlands. It is a great spot for birdwatching.

Access:
From Invermere drive towards Panorama. Just after crossing Toby creek turn right and go 2 km until you reach Wilmer. Turn right onto Main Street which turns to gravel at the north end of Wilmer and becomes Westside Road. Park after
1.9 km on the right near some interpretive signs.

Trail:
There are several trails in this area. A popular option is to head downhill from the parking area along the top of the cliffs to the narrow spit of land  overlooking the wetland, then turning north along the shore before circling back through the open woods and climbing back up to the parking area.

7 Lake Enid

Distance: 2 km
Time: 30 minutes
Elevation Gain: 20 m
Map Page 87

A short hike around a beautiful little lake. The lake is popular for swimming, fishing, and camping. If you are lucky, you may also see western painted turtles.

Lake Enid

Access:
From Invermere drive towards Panorama. Just after crossing the Toby Creek bridge turn right and go 2 km to reach Wilmer. Turn right on Main Street and then left on Park Street. This turns into a gravel road at the edge of town and becomes Horsethief Road. The road follows Wilmer Lake (Munn Lake) and goes around some fields. After the 4 km sign the road climbs slightly and becomes quite rough. After another 2 kilometers take the road to the right which leads to the Lake Enid Recreation Site.

Trail:
From the parking area go left behind a campsite. Cross a bridge by the outlet. Follow the shoreline on a nice trail and eventually reach a dirt road on the other side of the lake. Follow the dirt road around the lake. Cross the inlet on another bridge and then look for the trail on the right going back into the woods. There is a boardwalk and some interpretive signs here.

8 Old Coach and Deja Vu

Distance: 15.4 km
Time: 4 hours
Elevation Gain: 413 m

View of the wetlands from Deja Vu Trail

The Old Coach trail is a doubletrack road which leads to Radium from the trailhead. The Deja Vu trail is a single track which follows along the top of the cliffs overlooking the wetland. Together they make a fine loop. Shorter options also exist.

Access:
The Old coach parking lot is located 7 km north of Invermere or 6.4 km south of Radium on the west side of the highway. The parking lot is well signed.

Trail:
Leaving the trailhead climb up and over a small ridge. When you reach the Old Coach Road, turn left. After a hundred meters look for a single track to the right. Follow this trail and eventually it leads to the edge of the cliffs overlooking the wetlands. It meanders along for a couple kilometers before reaching the Old Coach Road again. You can turn right and return to the parking lot for a 4 km loop or continue left on the road, finding the trail again on the left after crossing the ravine. This section is quite short before it rejoins the Old Coach Road. The trail starts again on the left after 50 m. The

next section is also short. Reach the road again and again look for trail on the left after 50 m. The next section of single track is about 2 km. Then walk on the Old Coach Road for 100 m before taking the deja vu trail again for another 1 km. At this point the trail crosses the road. You can take a left and continue on the old coach trail all the way to Radium or turn right and return on the Old Coach Road to the parking lot.

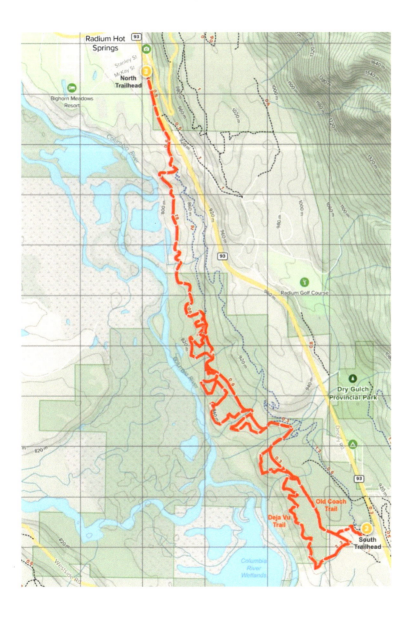

9 Juniper Sinclair Loop

Distance: 7.7km
Time: 2 hours
Elevation Gain: 281 m

This is a short hike which goes right below the highway and then climbs above the red rock canyon near the Radium Hot Springs, giving a unique perspective to a canyon you have probably driven through many times.

Sinclair Canyon from the Juniper - Sinclair trail

Access:
Park at the hot springs parking lot, just up the hill from the town of Radium.

Trail:

An old road leads above the parking lot. Follow it for a short distance before taking a trail on the left. This climbs up through the open forest and then contours well above the canyon. Eventually it starts dropping down again and ends up crossing Sinclair Creek. After crossing the creek be sure to take the short detour upstream to see the waterfall below the highway - invisible to drivers above. Rejoin the main trail and climb up to the road. Walk along the road for 150 m then cross - cautiously! - to the other side where a trail leads steeply up the bank. Continue on this trail, being sure to stop at the viewpoint overlooking the canyon. Eventually the trail becomes fairly wide and level before dropping back down to the hot springs.

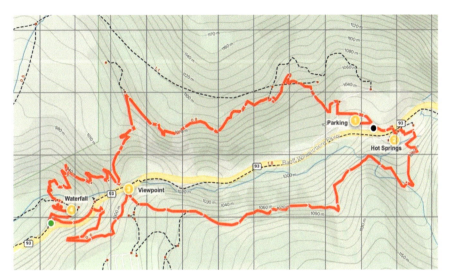

10 The Kloosifier

Distance: 7.6 km
Time: 2 hours
Elevation Gain: 240 m

This trail is mainly used by mountain bikers but also makes an excellent trail run or short hike. It is very close to town and has great views of the Toby Creek Canyon.

Hoodoos on the Kloosifier Trail

Access:
From Invermere drive towards Panorama. After crossing Toby Creek, drive up Peters Hill. At the top of the hill take the first right into the parking lot.

Trail:
Cross the road to reach the trail. The usual direction is to go counterclockwise: Take the right fork at the first junction. The trail meanders through open grassland and shrubland, eventually reaching the canyon rim. The trail goes along the rim to a hairpin turn with a bench which makes a nice spot for a break. It then continues downhill. There are easier and harder options in a couple spots. Eventually the trail levels out before reaching a double track road. Go up this for a short section before regaining the trail. Eventually the trail starts climbing up again and crests the height of land. It

drops down, crosses a fence and returns to the start. The trail can also be connected with the Johnson (hike #11) for a 20 km loop.

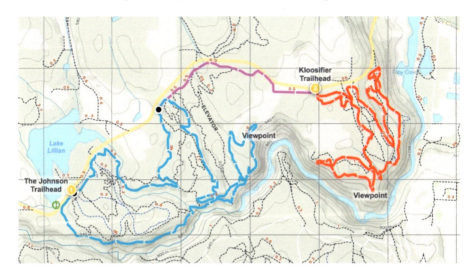

Lake Lillian trail network trailhead

11 The Johnson

Distance: 9.5 km
Time: 2-3 hours
Elevation Gain: 378 m

The Lake Lillian trails are a multi-use network for hiking, mountain biking, or trail running. In the winter trails are groomed for fat biking and cross country skiing. The Classic Johnson is a well signed 10 km loop which goes along the Toby Creek Canyon.

Access:
From Invermere drive towards Panorama. About 5 km from Invermere look for a parking area and small lake on the right. Park here and cross the road to access the trail network.

Trail:
Many options exist. One suggested route starts left of the trail kiosk, on Junior Johnson. Where Junior Johnson meets the Johnson trail, go straight on Johnson and continue descending slightly. At the creek turn left and cross the bridge. Continue on the Johnson trail - the intersections are all well signed. Eventually you come out along the edge of the canyon. The trail follows the canyon for several kilometers.

Eventually the trail goes back into the forest and returns to the trail head. You can also combine the Johnson and Kloosifier trails for a 20 km loop.

12 Valley Trail

Distance: 4 km
Time: 1.5 h
Elevation Gain: 160 m

This short, paved trail at Panorama is a good shoulder season or rainy day walk. It has a nice section along Toby Creek.

Access:
Park at the lower Panorama parking lot, near the adventure center/tennis courts.

Trail:
The trail starts behind the adventure center. Turn right before the bridge and walk on the paved trail along the creek. After half a kilometer the trail crosses the creek. It continues along the creek before climbing up beside the golf course. Cross the road and go past the clubhouse where the trail continues on the other side of the pond. It ends at the base of the ski hill. You can either take the free village gondola back to the lower parking lot or take the stairs.

13 Fairmont Trails

Fairmont Hot Springs has a network of short trails which are great for shoulder season hiking. Some of the trails can be combined into longer outings.

Trailhead 1 (Hot Springs Resort)

A Owls Loop
Distance: 2.8 km Rating: easy--moderate
This popular hike meanders through mature Douglas fir forest and connects with the Geary Lookout. Follow the trail markers carefully when you reach a large open field. Recommended loop: combine with Geary lookout or Columbia Lake

B Montezuma's Revenge
Distance: 1.5 km Rating: Moderate
This multi-use trail weaves through fairly tight forest. Intermediate bike stunts can be walked around. It is recommended that hikers go clockwise as bikers go counter-clockwise.

C Geary Lookout
Distance: 1.2 km Rating: easy
This trail starts high on the bluff of mountainside golf course. From the lookout you can see across the valley to the Hoodoos. The trail starts along the upper edge of the Fairmont Creek canyon and goes south along an old road to the RV park. Recommended: Combine with Waterfall Trail for a loop.

D Holland Loop
Distance: 1.4 km Rating: easy-moderate
This short hike wanders through open grassland and offers views of the Columbia Valley. It starts across from site 136 in the RV park however please park outside the RV park and walk in

E Overlook Trail
Distance: 0.5 km Rating: easy-moderate
This trail connects Fairmont Hot Springs to Fairmont ridge/ Marble Canyon condos. It follows the top of Fairmont Creek Canyon. It can be connected with Geary Lookout trail and Waterfall trail however it requires crossing the creek on rocks. Do not attempt the crossing when the water is high.

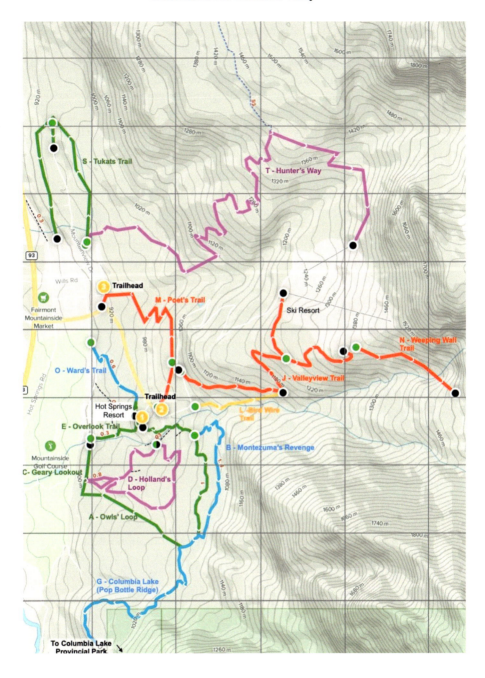

F Columbia Lake (Pop Bottle Ridge)

Distance: 3+ km Rating: moderate

This trail offers spectacular views of Columbia Lake and wetlands. You can continue to Columbia Lake Provincial Park along an unmaintained trail. This can be combined with the Spirit Trail. Start from trailhead 1 along Owl Loop

Trailhead 2 (across the parking lot from Hot Springs Resort)

J Valleyview Trail

Distance 3.3 km Rating: moderate

Ski hill connector 0.6 km

This trail takes you from the resort on a footpath past the historical baths onto an old road to the ski hill. You can either take the ski hill connector to the base of the ski hill or keep climbing to come out higher up on the ski hill. Valleyview offers amazing views of the valley and an abundance of wildflowers in the summer.

L Bird Wire Trail

Distance 1.2 km Rating: moderate

This multi-use trail travels through mature forest along a canyon edge. It is mainly used by mountain bikers.

M Poet Trail

Distance 1.8 km Rating: moderate

This wide switch back trail connects the resort lodge with the lower town site. Enjoy various poems posted on trees along the route. There is no bridge over the creek. You must cross on rocks. Do not attempt this when the water is high.

N Weeping Wall Trail

Distance: varies Rating: moderate

This short trail at the top of the ski hill follows a pumphouse service road and then ends abruptly. You can scramble up a creek to discover a cold water spring flowing from the mountain. Continue to a waterfall at the end of the trail. Do not attempt this hike when water levels are high.

O Ward's Trail

Distance 0.9 km Rating: moderate

This trail can be used to connect the resort lodge with Mountainside Golf Course. The views of the golf course make it a pleasant alternative to walking on the road.

Valleyview Trail

Trailhead 3 (Mountain Ridge Road)

S Tukats Trail
Distance 2.3 km rating easy-moderate
This forested trail is a peaceful walk to the Nighthawk viewpoint. From where you can see the Columbia River, the wetlands and Lake Windermere. During the summer evenings listen for the sound of the nighthawks though watch your step as they nest on the ground.

T Hunters Way
Distance 5.2 km Rating Moderate
This trail follows seldom used ATV tracks high into the hills. Look down on the valley and ski area from numerous viewpoints.

14 Lower Bugaboo Falls

Distance: 2.9 km
Time: 2 hours
Elevation Gain: 135 m

This is a great short hike to some impressive waterfalls. Be careful near the falls as there are no safety fences. Keep an eye on children and dogs.

Access:
From Radium drive 28 km north to Brisco. Turn Left on Brisco Road (before the gas station/general store). Continue for 8.4 km where Brisco Road merges with Westside Road. Continue north. Go another 3.1 km and you will see the parking spot on the left side.

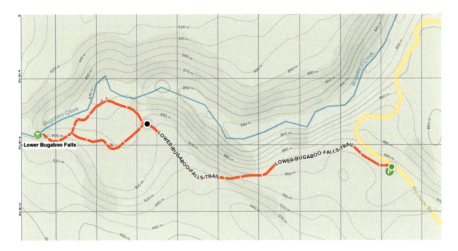

Trail:
The trail starts above the road. It wanders through the trees before coming to the falls. You will likely hear them before you see them!

Lower Bugaboo Falls. Photo: Cam Mclellan

15 Marion Benchlands

Distance: 11.5 km
Time: 2-3 hours
Elevation Gain: 285 m

The area west of Columbia Lake is a patchwork of protected lands. There are many decommissioned roads and trails which make for pleasant walking in open forest and grasslands. The following is a recommended route but many other options exist.

Access:
From Fairmont drive south for 12 km and turn right on Hardie Creek Road. Drive up the hill and park on the right in a flat spot after about 200 m.

Trail:
Start on an old road which climbs up the hill on the right, through recently logged forest. Just after the fence there is a trail on the left, which eventually enters more dense forest and meanders along the rim of the canyon. Shortly after crossing a distinct gully the trail merges onto an old road. After 20 m on this road the trail continues on the left. Eventually the trail comes out

onto another old road. Turn left and walk down the road for 1 km. Here you can either continue down the old road back to the trailhead, through a pleasant forested valley or, for a slightly longer version, climb up a trail on the right which gains the ridge on the other side of the valley. Look for the trail shortly after another road merges from the right, in a fairly wide open meadow. The trail continues along the rim of the valley for about 1 km before coming out into an open area and eventually leads to an old road. You get glimpses of Columbia Lake through the trees and nice views of the Fairmont Range. Turn left on the road as it descends back to the valley. Turn right when it rejoins the other road and follow it back to the start.

Marion Benchlands

FINDLAY CREEK

16 Doctor Creek

Distance: 12-14 km
Time: 3-4 hours
Elevation Gain: 500-600 m

The Doctor Creek area is made up of several remote subalpine basins just east of the Purcell Wilderness Conservancy. The lower Doctor Creek valley was burnt by a large forest fire in 2020, however the area described here was spared. There are two snowmobile cabins, as well as spots to camp. There

are multiple small tarns in the area and several options for hiking. Hiking the ridge to the west of the basin is great, as you get fantastic views of the high peaks of the Purcells Wilderness to the west and St. Mary's Alpine Provincial Park to the south. The valley around the cabin and the higher lake also offers plenty to explore.

Access:
The upper Doctor Creek road is quite rough, and a 4WD with high clearance is recommended. Take the Findlay Creek FSR, which is 2.5 km north of Canal Flats. Set your odometer here. Note that the yellow kilometer markers start at 3 km. For clarity's sake we will use odometer readings here rather than the yellow markers. Follow the main Findlay Creek road. Stay left at 12.7km, the right road goes to Whitetail Lake. At 18.6 km cross a bridge and at 21.5 km take the left road which is marked Doctor Creek. At 22.1 km stay left. You will now enter the burnt forest and descend to a canyon. It is awe inspiring to drive through this recent burn, and also interesting to see how quickly some plants grow back as part of the natural forest fire cycle. At 32.5 km the road gets very rough. At 34.7 km the road is washed out and only an ATV will make it through this section. If at some point the road gets fixed, you may be able to drive further up the valley.

Trail:
Continue past the washout for another 1.4 km. The road forks here and you have to decide which direction you want to take. There are two main options - the hardest thing may be deciding which to take because they are both great.

Tarn above Doctor Creek Cabin

Option 1 - Doctor Cabin and Doctor Lake

Take the left road which deteriorates into a narrower ATV track. At 3.3 km from the trailhead take the more obviously travelled road left and shortly afterwards cross the creek. The cabin is only 200 m further down the road. You will see it from a bend in the road. This single room cabin has a loft, benches, a wood stove and a fair share of mouse droppings. It sits at the edge of a lovely meadow ringed by granite peaks, and surrounded by tall trees. It is a great spot. To continue up to Doctor Lake, go back to the bend in the road and continue uphill. You will soon pass by a mine shaft and the remains of a cabin. If you look over the edge of the road you will see remnants of an old truck. Do not go into the mine shaft - it could be unstable. Continue uphill. After another kilometer the road tops out. Take the left steep ATV trail as it continues to climb up through larch forest. This ATV trail continues past treeline and into a talus bowl where it peters out. You will be able to see Doctor Lake below you. It is an unusual shade of blue. You can turn back here or continue to ridgetop from where you get great views of Greenland Creek to the south. You can continue along the ridge in either direction for some distance. Returning down the ATV trail, take the next left which will take you to the lake. Continue along the creek canyon and hike past another snowmobile cabin. There is another road which goes left and downhill to the creek before climbing up the other side. However, to return to the valley take the right which soon leads back to the spot where you took the steep ATV track uphill. Walk back down on the old mine road and return to the trailhead the way you came.

Option 2- Upper Doctor Creek

Take the right road which soon crosses the creek and continues up the valley, becoming narrower. After 5 km from the junction the trail peters out. Continue up the valley into open meadows. Pass by a couple small tarns as you head for the ridgeline at the head of the valley, 1.5 km from the end of the trail. It is easily gained. From the ridge you get fantastic views of the headwaters of Findlay Creek and the high peaks of the Purcells to the west.

Other Options: There is another, larger lake between the two basins. It is accessed via a branch off the road, 1.8 km from the junction and then some off trail travel.

17 Findlay Creek to Morigeau Basin

Distance: 66 km
Time: multiday
Elevation Gain: 900 m

Findlay Creek leads into the heart of the Purcell Wilderness Conservancy. It is a wild and remote area and this trip should only be attempted by experienced mountain travelers. The chance of seeing bears and other wildlife is high. The access trail is long, and requires multiple unbridged river crossings. It is mainly a horse trail maintained by a guide outfitter who has a cabin at the confluence of Findlay and Granite Creeks, used in the fall for hunting. While the Findlay valley itself is beautiful, the real prize is the high country around Findlay Peak and the Lee and Clutterbuck group, which are high glaciated granite peaks. The Granite and Morigeau valleys are remote alpine basins where you will be rewarded with solitude and beautiful mountain scenery. Several peaks can be climbed from Morigeau Basin, including Trikootenay, Findlay, Rowand and Morigeau. Trikootenay Peak is a hydrographic apex, draining into Kootenay Lake to the west, the Columbia River via Dutch Creek, and the Kootenay River via Findlay Creek. It is a moderate scramble. Alpine climbers will be able to make ascents in the Lees and Clutterbuck group from Granite Creek.

Looking up the Findlay Creek Valley towards the Purcell Wilderness (note the absence of cut blocks)

Access:

Take the Findlay Creek FSR, which is 2.5 km north of Canal Flats. Set your odometer here. Note that the yellow kilometer markers start at 3 km. For clarity's sake we will use odometer readings from the highway turnoff rather than the yellow markers. Follow the main Findlay Creek road. Stay left at 12.7 km, the right road goes to Whitetail Lake. At 18 km, turn right on Valentine Creek FSR, follow this road for 8.1 km to the trailhead. The trail goes over a washout. Valentine Creek FSR is rough and rutted, 4 WD and high clearance is required.

Morigeau Basin and Mount Findlay

Trail:

Follow a decent horse trail. There are boggy sections and many unbridged river crossings. It is about 24.5 km to the outfitter cabin near the confluence of Granite and Findlay creek, where a small meadow nearby makes a good spot to camp. The next day, hike up Granite Creek until the junction with Morigeau creek about 3.5 km. Take the right fork, climbing through forest and eventually into large avalanche paths as the country opens up. It is about 8.5 km from the cabin to the upper basin at Morigeau Creek. There is nice camping in the basin. It is worthwhile spending a few days exploring this area and scrambling the nearby peaks. Alternatively, continue up the Granite creek valley to access the Lee and Clutterbuck group. It is about 10 km from the cabin to the basin.

BREWER CREEK

18 Brewer Lakes

Distance: 10 km
Time: 3-4 hours
Elevation Gain: 450 m

The Brewer lakes area is a beautiful basin with flowers and tarns. It is a fairly short but rewarding hike. It is also possible to scramble Mount Brewer or to continue to Ben Abel Lake from here.

Access:

From Invermere drive 18 km south on Westside Road to Hawke Road. Turn right at a large parking area with the Hoodoo kiosk on your right. Continue 26 km to the trailhead, staying on the main dirt road for 11 km until you come to a fork in the road. Go straight (the other fork goes left) up a slight hill for 0.5 km before taking a less traveled road going left. There should be a Brewer Creek sign here. Continue on this road to the trailhead. For the last 2 km of road you need a high-clearance 4-wheel drive vehicle. It takes about 1 hour from Invermere.

Trail:

For the first 2 km the trail parallels Brewer Creek in the trees, gaining 240 meters before breaking out into an open meadow. After 5 km you reach the first tarn. From there the trail to the right will take you to another tarn a short distance away. If you continue on this trail you can gain the Mount Brewer ridge (see hike # 19). The trail continues to Hopeful Pass and eventually all the way to Panorama (see hike #24). Going left at the first tarn for another 1.5 km will take you up onto a ridge at the end of the valley. From the ridge, looking back to the east you get a great view of Brewer Basin, to the west you look down on one of the tributaries that feed Mineral Creek and north to Mount Nelson and the Delphine Glacier. There are spots to camp at the lake.

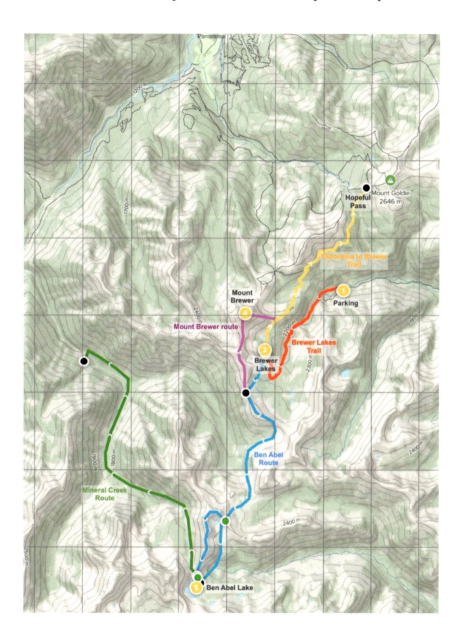

19 Mount Brewer

Distance: 12.9 km
Time: 4-5 hours
Elevation Gain: 959 m

The Mount Brewer scramble is excellent, and not overly difficult. From the summit you can see the high glaciated peaks to the west in the Earl Grey pass area and the Jumbo area as well as an eye level view of Mount Nelson to the north.

Access:
See Brewer Creek hike.

Summit of Mount Brewer

Trail:
From Brewer Lake hike past the second tarn on the trail that leads to Hopeful Pass (to the northeast). When the trail crosses the east ridge of Mount Brewer, start climbing up the ridge. It is fairly straightforward up to the summit. You can either return the way you came or descend via the west ridge to a col, climb up and over the next peak and continue to the ridge at the head of Brewer Basin where you will find a trail back to the tarns. This is a fantastic ridge walk with some easy scrambling. The views of the Purcell Wilderness are fantastic.

20 Ben Abel Lake

Distance: 28 km (8 km one way from Brewer Lake)
Time: 2 days (5 hours from Brewer Lake)
Elevation Gain: 1000-1150 m (high level and low level option)

Ben Abel Lake is a stellar backpacking trip to a remote sparkling blue lake with good fishing. There are two ways to access Ben Abel. The hike from Brewer Lakes is a beautiful alpine and subalpine route, through flower filled meadows. A faint trail is present for most of the way but some routefinding skills are required. The access from Mineral Creek is a valley bottom struggle up a difficult horse trail. For obvious reasons we recommend the route from Brewer Lakes. It is worth spending a few days exploring and enjoying this beautiful area.

Access:
See Brewer Creek hike.

Trail:
From Brewer Lake continue along a trail to the left of the first lake which climbs slightly along the base of the mountain before dropping down again. At a junction stay right to gain the ridge at the end of the valley. If you go left you end up at another tarn. Follow the ridge, scoping the route to Ben Abel in the valley below. After the high point on the ridge start descending the other side. The slope below some white colored rocks is least steep but

take caution as you descend on loose steep terrain. When you reach the flats below follow a little creek. Where the terrain steepens traverse slightly right then left again. When you reach a little tarn follow it to the other end. The route to Ben Abel is marked in spots with cairns and flagging and there is a faint trail however if you keep the edge of the talus slope on your left and the forest on your right you should have no problems finding the trail. Eventually the trail enters the forest and may be harder to find. As you round the corner you will see the pass above, ascend through meadows in open forest to the pass. From the pass climb up steeply for about 30 meters to the right to gain a broad plateau. Here you have two options.

Fishing at Ben Abel Lake

For an easier option continue to the low spot on the ridge ahead and descend on the other side towards a small tarn, follow a creek into a small canyon and then stay left of the creek as you drop elevation. Eventually you will see a trail climbing out of the canyon up the other side, this trail contours around the mountain side and eventually gains a slope to the meadows below Ben Abel Lake.

For a more difficult but scenic options, climb the ridge to the right of the low point. Enjoy views of the Delphine Glacier and Mount Nelson to the north. From the high point above the ridge ahead looks daunting and knife edged but as you work along you realize the backside is easier than it looks. Follow this ridge along as it eventually drops all the way to Ben Abel Lake.

There are several campsites at the north end of the lake.

Ben Abel Lake. The high level approach descends the ridge in the background.

Options:

One could spend days exploring the area around the lake, from the meadow and waterfall below the outlet to the ridge above the inlet. The hike to the dark grey ridge above the inlet (south end of the lake) is pleasant and fairly short. Follow the lakeside trail all the way around and then climb easily through flower meadows to scree slopes above. Follow a horse trail to the ridge from where you can enjoy views of the Dutch Creek drainage and the Purcell wilderness. 1 hour from lake

Mineral Creek to Ben Abel

Mineral Creek can be used to access Ben Abel Lake. It can also be combined with the Panorama to Brewer and Brewer to Ben Abel hike to make it a 3-day backpacking trip, but why would you? Unless you are really opposed to backtracking this option is not recommended. It is a rough pack trail and often hard to follow, and it is only slightly better than bushwhacking. It follows a steep enclosed valley bottom and requires multiple fords. Views are limited until you are almost at Ben Abel Lake. Considering the alternative approach to Ben Abel is an amazing alpine ramble filled with vistas and flowers, Mineral Creek is better left to horse packers. If you insist, here is the description:

From Ben Abel Lake:
Climb the pass to the north of the lake. Pick up the horse trail as it descends on the right side of the valley, staying high above another small tarn. The trail frequently becomes indistinct but when in doubt stay to the right of the valley as you lose elevation. You can follow the creek in a small gorge but watch for a horse trail on the right bank just as the creek becomes steeper. Continue on this horse trail as it crosses numerous avalanche paths and stands of mature timber. The trail is often hard to follow in the avalanche paths but when in doubt it is usually higher on the slope and does not come near the creek until valley bottom. Once in the valley the trail becomes much easier to follow and crosses the creek several times. Eventually you pass an outfitters cabin. At this point you must cross the creek again on some logs. You are now on the east side of the valley where the trail goes through many avalanche paths. The going is quite tedious with lots of deadfall and rocks to stumble over. Eventually the trail crosses the creek again. The crossing is easier on some rocks about 20 m upstream from the horse trail but be sure to rejoin the horse trail as it climbs steeply through open forest, and eventually mature timber to a landing. 4-5 hours, 14 km, 1150 m elevation loss

From Toby Creek:
From the end of pavement drive 13.7 km on the Toby Creek FSR. Take the Coppercrown FSR on your left. Stay on the main road, ignoring any junctions by staying right. You should end up on the highest of the logging roads in the cut blocks, which eventually drops down slightly again and then dead ends. From the end of the drivable road walk to the end of the skid road and look for the trail as it goes into the tall trees. The trail drops very steeply to the creek through some mature timber and eventually open slopes. Important: after crossing the creek walk downstream for about 20 metres to pick up the horse trail. It is a rough trail that follows the east side of the valley until you cross the creek again and reach the outfitters cabin. 6-8 hours, 14 km, 1150 m elevation gain.

PANORAMA

The Panorama area offers beautiful hiking in subalpine and alpine terrain. The catch is that you have to hike uphill through the ski resort to get there. You can lessen the pain by taking the Mile 1 chairlift, but it is still a good uphill walk from the top of the lift. If at some point summer lift access goes to the top of the Champagne Express lift, the hiking at Panorama will likely be a lot more appealing to the masses. In the meantime, there are great uncrowded hikes for those willing to put in the effort. Please be aware that the Panorama Controlled Recreation Area may be closed to hiking at certain times of year. Check the website for updates.

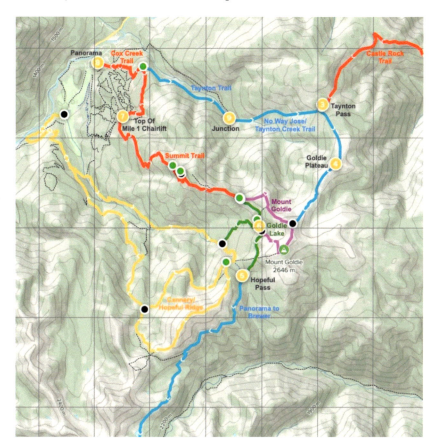

Hiking access to the summit/Taynton Ridge:
From the bottom of the Mile 1 chairlift go left to find the Cox Creek Trail. Follow it uphill for 3.2 km gaining 400 m elevation. Then take the Lynx trail, to the top of the Mile 1 lift after another 0.5 km. Alternatively, pay for a one-

ride lift ticket. From the top of the Mile 1 lift take the Summit Trail which goes another 3.4 km gaining 600 m elevation to the top of the Champagne Chair. From there, find the Summit Uptrack which starts behind the winter trail map. It is 1.4 km long and gains another 115 m. It ends in a road which leads to the summit. To get to Taynton Ridge go straight at the next switchback. If you go left, you will end up at the Summit Hut. One way distance is 9.1 km to the summit ridge with 1205 m elevation gain. If you take the chairlift, the one-way distance is 5.4 km with 779 m elevation gain.

21 Mount Goldie

Distance: 14 km (add 7.4 km without chairlift)
Time: 6-8 hours
Elevation Gain: 1100 m (add 426 m without chairlift)

Mount Goldie is the prominent peak visible from the Panorama summit. It is an easy scramble and is worthwhile for its fantastic views of the Purcells, the Rockies, and the Columbia Valley. It can be combined with Goldie Lake for a stellar, but long day.

Access: Via Taynton Ridge

Trail:
Follow the road along Taynton ridge and climb up to the top of the Monster ski run. From here follow the ridge through subalpine meadows and open larch forest to the base of Mount Goldie. Easy scrambling leads up the ridge to the summit of Mount Goldie. After enjoying the views of the Rockies and Purcells, including Mount Nelson and Assiniboine, you can return the way you came. For a slightly longer option, continue along the ridge and descend the far end towards Goldie Lake. From the lake take the McKay trail back up to Taynton ridge and return to the base of the ski resort the way you came up.

22 Goldie Lake

Distance: 15.5 km (add 7.4 km without chairlift)
Time: 6-8 hours
Elevation Gain: 895 m (add 426 m without chairlift)

Goldie Lake is a beautiful tarn tucked below Mount Goldie. It is a refreshing dip on a hot day.

Access: Via Taynton Ridge

Trail:

Follow Taynton ridge to the end. Shortly after it begins climbing up towards the Monster ski run, take the McKay trail on the right. Follow this trail through subalpine meadows as it drops slightly. At the marked junction go left to reach Goldie Lake in a few hundred meters. Return the same way or take the Hopeful Creek Trail back, to make a loop. To get to the Hopeful Creek trail, continue on McKay past Goldie Lake for 1.5 km until you reach Hopeful Pass, then turn right onto the Hopeful Creek trail. This trail is 6.4 km long and ends on a cat road. Turn right on the cat road to find your way back to the resort, about 2 km from the end of the Hopeful trail. Be sure not to stray onto any downhill bike trails as you make your way back!

23 Goldie Plateau via Taynton Creek (No Way Jose Trail)

Distance: 18 km
Time: 5-7 hours
Elevation Gain: 1300 m

Goldie Plateau is a broad open plateau between Mount Taynton and Mount Goldie. It is a beautiful alpine ramble with views of Mount Nelson and the Columbia Valley. Once you leave the pass behind, there is no distinct trail but it is easy route finding through open larch forest. In the fall, the colors are spectacular. Goldie Plateau can be combined with an ascent of Mount Goldie.

Looking across the valley on the Goldie Plateau

Access:
Panorama ski resort.

Trail:
From the base of the ski hill hike up the Cox Creek trail, which starts just left of the bottom of the Mile 1 lift. Follow it for 1.8 km until it intersects the Taynton trail cat road. About 2.5 km up the Taynton trail, look for a single track trail to the left called No Way Jose (also called Taynton Creek Trail). In the winter this is the ski out from the run Wild Thing. Go up this trail, crossing the creek after a short distance. The trail now steadily gains elevation for about an hour until you reach a pass. If you continue straight along the pass the trail eventually connects with the Castle Rock Trail which is a long and scenic option and requires a car shuttle (see Castle Rock, Hike #26). To gain Goldie Plateau hike up through open larch forest from the pass. The trail is fairly indistinct. Continue gaining elevation until you break out of the forest. You can amble along the pleasant open plateau, enjoying the views. If you want, connect with the east ridge of Mount Goldie to the summit, returning via the Panorama summit trail for a longer option. Otherwise return

the same way you came up. This hike is especially pleasant in the fall when the larches are in full color.

Larches on the Goldie Plateau

Hiking to Taynton Pass on the way to Goldie Plateau
Photo: Cam Mclellan

24 Panorama to Brewer

Distance: 15.4 km one way (add 3.7 km if not taking chairlift)
Time: 6-8 hours one way
Elevation Gain: 1195 m (add 426 m if not taking chairlift)

This is an interesting option to connect the two areas. With a car shuttle you could make this a point to point hike. This trail can also be used to access Ben Abel Lake from Panorama, which would take two days in one direction and is an excellent option.

Panorama to Brewer Trail with Mount Brewer in the background

Access:
Start at the top of Taynton Ridge.

Trail:

From Taynton Ridge at the top of Panorama continue along until the McKay trail branches off to the right. Follow it downhill for a short distance. Be sure to take the short detour to Goldie Lake. Continuing along the McKay trail, it starts gaining elevation again before dropping down to Hopeful Pass. At the pass there are some old cabins which are not in good condition anymore. Take the trail to the left which contours around the mountain side for several kilometers before breaking out into a meadow. From the meadow continue uphill a short way, passing a slight depression in the ground. Climb up the hillside past this depression to find the trail to Brewer again. The trail continues through open meadows, eventually passing the first Brewer Lake. The second, bigger lake is a short distance beyond. It has several good spots to camp though there are no facilities.

Historic McKay Cabins at Hopeful Pass

25 Hopeful Ridge (Cannery)

Distance: 25 km
Time: 8-10 hours
Elevation Gain: 1590 m

This is a spectacular ridge walk with fantastic views. It is close to Panorama yet it is unlikely you will see anyone else. It is a long day but very worthwhile. You can use a bike for the first few kilometers and make the hike shorter.

Cannery/Hopeful Ridge

Access:
Drive past the Greywolf Golf course and park just before the bridge.

Trail:
Cross the bridge and go downhill on the wide cross country ski trail. It parallels the creek for a while then goes up and over a small hill. At the first major road stay left (Alder trail). This road starts climbing up above the Nordic center. It switchbacks left, then right. After 1.4 km stay left. After another 500 m stay left and descend slightly to Hopeful Creek. The right fork will be the way you come back. If you are using a bike, leave it here. After crossing Hopeful Creek look for a single track on the right. The trail climbs steeply before levelling out. It ascends pleasantly through open forest and

crosses several small creeks Beware that this trail is used by mountain bikers. Continue following Hopeful Creek. Stay left at the first junction, then right at the next junction. Just before reaching the height of land at Hopeful Pass take a faint trail to the right at a four-way intersection. The trail goes through some small tight trees. Keep an eye out for another trail going uphill on the left after about 150m. Take this trail for 300 meters then look for another faint trail going up the ridge as the trees start opening up. Continue gaining elevation. As you break out of the trees, continue going uphill along the ridge.

You are now on the Cannery ridge proper. Meander along the ridgeline, enjoying the views of Mount Nelson to the north, Assiniboine to the East and even glimpses of Columbia Lake to the south. The further along you go the better the views get and eventually you reach a high point from where you can see the glaciers of Earl Grey Pass and Jumbo Pass to the west. From the summit continue along the ridge to the west and scramble down on loose rocks, picking your way along until you reach the flats below. Continue all the way to the low spot on the ridge and look for a trail going right. This trail descends through open larch forest to the basin below where it eventually ends up at an outfitter cabin. From the cabin continue on the trail to the left which goes uphill slightly before descending through the forest. At a junction stay left going downhill. The trail continues downhill through the forest before eventually turning left onto an old overgrown road bed. Continue along this road bed for a while, crossing a small creek and eventually reaching the junction with the Nordic center road. Continue downhill, along the switchbacks and back to the flats at the bottom. Return to the parking lot the way you came.

26 Castle Rock Trail

Distance: 8.5 km
Time: 3-4 hours
Elevation Gain: 690 m

Castle Rock is a prominent mountain feature just west of Invermere. A steep but good trail leads to the Castle Rock view point. Access is complicated by the fact that the road to the trailhead passes through Zehnder Farm which is private property. However, the road is public. Please be courteous when driving through the farm. The Castle Rock trail can be hiked all the way to Panorama by connecting with the Mount Taynton trail to Goldie Plateau.

Access:
From Invermere take Westside Road and turn right on Johnson Road after 500 m. Follow Johnson Road to the end, then turn left onto Zehnder Farm. Continue through the farm, all the way to the end of the road and park by the yellow gate before the power line.

Trail:
Cross the powerline and walk up the road directly opposite the parking area. After a few hundred meters you come to the trail kiosk and the official start of the trail. The trail switchbacks up the dry open forest. Once the trail finally levels out there is a good view point. Continue uphill. Where the trail goes into a ravine, look for a faint trail to the right. This trail will take you to the Castle Rock viewpoint which you reach after a few hundred meters. Be careful not to lose your footing near the edge as there is quite a drop off. Enjoy the panoramic views of the Columbia Valley before returning the way you came.

Lake Windermere from Castle Rock Trail.
Photo: Cam Mclellan

Option:
You can continue all the way to Panorama. From the ravine, take the left trail and continue via the flanks of Mount Taynton to Taynton Pass and eventually to Panorama, either by dropping down to Taynton Creek or continuing via Goldie Plateau and Mount Goldie to the summit of Panorama (see hikes #23 and #21). It is 23 km one way, with 1630 m elevation gain from the Castle Rock Trail to the Panorama base, via the Mount Goldie summit.

TOBY CREEK – JUMBO CREEK

27 Mount Nelson

Distance: 10.4 km
Time: 8-10 hours
Elevation Gain: 1897 m

This is the prominent peak to the west of Invermere. It was named by David Thompson after the British admiral who defeated Napoleon's navy at the battle of Trafalgar. It should only be attempted by experienced scramblers. It is a long day and requires route finding. You should be fairly comfortable scrambling on loose rock. Wear a helmet and avoid knocking rocks onto those below you.

Scrambling near the summit of Mount Nelson on a smoky day in July

Access:

From Panorama continue on the Toby Creek FSR. Turn right on the Delphine FSR, 7.9km from the end of pavement. The first few hundred meters on this road are quite rough but it improves further along before ending at a washout, 1.9 km from the Toby FSR.

Trail:

Cross the washout. Look for a faint trail on the other side of the washout, going upstream. Initially it may be hard to find but if you stay on the left side

of the creek you should eventually intersect the trail. It starts climbing very steeply through open forest. After about an hour you reach a flat spot on the ridge which is a good spot for a break. The trail continues uphill for a few more minutes before descending right, off the ridge. Contour slightly downhill through the forest until you eventually break out into the open basin. From here follow the creek uphill, traveling through shale and rocky terrain. Finally, you reach the basin from where the climb starts. Turn right and climb scree and talus slopes towards several gullies. The leftmost gully is the easiest, though the

rocky shelves just to the right of the gully are a bit more solid. Then you reach a talus filled bowl. A broken rock buttress is on the right of this bowl. Stay just left of it until you are just below the summit cone. Stay right and follow a faint path to the summit. Return the way you came, taking care on the descent.

28 Thunderbird Mine

Distance: 15.6 km
Time: 5-6 hours
Elevation Gain: 970 m

The Thunderbird Mine was only in operation very briefly, from 1935 to 1936. A lot of effort was put into this mine for not much apparent gain. Several buildings still remain though they are increasingly derelict. A good mule path was constructed up to this lofty site, high above the Delphine valley, and it makes for an excellent hike with great views.

Access:
Continue past the Panorama resort on the Toby Creek FSR. Turn right on the Delphine FSR, 7.9 km from the end of pavement. The first few hundred meters on this road are quite rough but the road improves further along before ending at a washout, 1.9 km from the Toby FSR.

Delphine Valley from Thunderbird Mine

Trail:
Continue on the road past the washout. After 300 m there is a second washout. After about 1.3 km from the trailhead look for a somewhat faint trail on the right. It is directly across from a wide avalanche path, the second avalanche path on the left as you go up the valley. The start of the trail is marked by a cairn. Initially the trail is a bit overgrown but it soon becomes more obvious. The trail follows an old mule track and it was very well built. In places you can still see the rockwork that was done to build the trail up. At 2 km from the trailhead you cross a small creek and then continue winding up the dry open forest. As you gain elevation you get great views of Monument Peak across the valley. At 5 km you cross the first of several avalanche paths. The last path is the largest and it has carved a deep canyon

into the mountain side. The old mining cabin is visible above on the treed ridge. To get across the other side you have to climb down into the canyon on a steep and slippery slope before traversing the other side to the mine site. A rope attached to a tree may help.

Option:

The old powerhouse for the mine sits another 500 m higher on a rocky rib. It is possible to scramble up to this spot for a commanding view of the Delphine Valley. Experienced mountaineers can also climb Sultana Peak, high above the Thunderbird Mine, a difficult scramble.

The valley above the Thunderbird Mine

29 Delphine Glacier

Distance: 24 km
Time: 1-2 days
Elevation Gain: 1510 m

Though the Delphine Valley is close to Panorama, getting to Delphine Glacier feels like an adventure in a remote area. Mountain bikes can be used for the approach, and are a great alternative to an otherwise long walk on an old logging road. The last part of the trail, which is marked on some maps, is very overgrown and you should be comfortable with route finding and some easy scrambling. With a bike approach, this can be done as a day hike. However, because this is such a spectacular area you may want to spend a night or two.

The moraine below the Delphine Glacier

Access:
From Panorama continue on the Toby Creek FSR. Turn right on the Delphine FSR, 7.9km from the end of pavement. The first few hundred meters on this road are quite rough but the road improves further along before ending at a washout, 1.9 km from the Toby FSR.

Trail:
Hike or bike on the road past the washout. After 2.2 km you come to another washout section which is several hundred meters across. The road continues on the other side. After another 2 km, the road is very close to the creek and is partially eroded. Shortly after this, the road branches. Take the right branch. You can leave your bike here, or if you are an experienced mountain biker

you can continue riding for another 2 km, though you may need to push your bike up some of the steeper sections. Park at the switchback.

Looking at the Delphine Glacier

The trail goes straight here. At first it is hard to find and you may have to scramble over some fallen logs. As you enter the forest, the old trail is easier to follow. Cross an avalanche and re-enter the forest. When you come to an open area with multiple avalanche paths the faint trail peters out. Look up at the route ahead. Further ahead is a black cliff band. You will eventually want to go along the right side of this cliff band until you can traverse left through a ramp. To get there you have a couple options: you can stay right, traversing open slopes which become more and more overgrown and eventually reaching a creek bed or you can go left here and follow the creek. Shortly after the creek bed curves right, cross over and briefly thrash through some Christmas trees before the terrain opens up more. Climb up here towards the black rock band, gaining elevation fairly quickly. When you reach the ramp, traverse left. There may be some old ropes tied to trees. The rock is more solid than it looks and the moves are fairly easy. From the top of the ramp continue uphill on talus, to a ridge above, which leads to the lateral moraine. The glacier is now directly in front of you. Enjoy the views of the Delphine valley behind you and the glacier in front of you. To continue further up, drop down slightly, cross the flats and climb up a gully to the right, staying on the right side of a creek to gain a higher basin. This is a great spot to camp. The glacier is further up and left. Do not go onto the glacier unless you have the training and equipment.

30 Earl Grey Pass

Distance: 36 km (55 km if continuing to West Kootenays)
Time: minimum 2 days
Elevation Gain: 1315 m

The Earl Grey Pass trail is a great multi-day wilderness adventure deep into the Purcell Wilderness. The pass is named for the former Governor General of Canada whose hunting cabin still exists along the trail. The Earl had the cabin built in 1909, and spent a summer here with his family. It is worth

looking at the remains of the cabin and a sign has been erected nearby with more information.

The length of the entire trail is 55 km one way, from Argenta in the West Kootenays to Toby Creek, and it usually takes 4-5 days to do the full hike. To hike the entire trail requires a car shuttle and the two trailheads are separated by over 400 km! Some people have coordinated car shuttles with another hiking party going the opposite direction to avoid having to do the drive twice. There are five cable car crossings over Hamill Creek in the West Kootenays. Be sure to look at current trail information before venturing out as these cable cars are not always operational. Hiking to Earl Grey Pass as an out and back is logistically easier, shorter and gets you to the most scenic parts of the trail.

Access:
From Panorama, drive west on the Toby Creek FSR for 19 km. Just past the Jumbo Creek bridge go left for the Earl Grey Pass trailhead. There is a parking lot, outhouse, and trail kiosk right after the turnoff. You can drive to the actual trailhead 1.5 km further down the road.

Trail: From the parking lot take the obvious trail which follows Toby Creek. You will come across three large open avalanche paths. The Earl Grey Cabin sits at the edge of the second slide path, about 1 km from the trailhead. It is well signed and worth the short detour. From the open areas you can see glimpses of the glaciated peaks of Earl Grey Pass ahead. After 3 km you will reach Pharaoh Creek which you will have to ford, or skip across on rocks. At 7.6 km you will reach the Teepee Campsite. After another 1 km you will reach McKay Falls. A few hundred meters after McKay Falls there is an old fence, and shortly afterwards the trail splits. Be sure to take the right fork, which goes uphill to a large slide path. The left fork is a horse trail which goes to South Toby Creek. At this point the trail starts contouring around the valley which was once known as Bannock Basin and it crosses several large slide paths with lush vegetation. Pass Toby Falls 6 km after McKay Falls. The trail now continues climbing, passing the outflow plains of the Toby Glacier,

which is a good spot to camp. Past the outflow, the trail switchbacks up to the pass. There are spots to camp at the pass - but no water. Be sure to fill up at one of the small creeks below the pass.

Mount Toby and Mount Hamill, from Blockhead Mountain.
Photo: Cam Mclellan

Options:
Scrambling Slate Peak, which is directly north of the pass, is highly recommended. It is worth going even part way up for excellent views of Mount Toby and the Hamill Glacier. Faint trails and cairns lead to the summit.

31 Black Diamond Basin

Distance: 16 km
Time: 4-6 hours
Elevation Gain: 1025 m

This trail follows an old roadbed high into a beautiful alpine basin. In the summer there are wildflowers galore and the fall colors are splendid. Waterfalls pour off the cliffs on either side of the valley. From the end of the

road, you can either scramble up to a pass overlooking the Farnham drainage, or climb up to another pass which looks into the Delphine Valley. Looking back, you get great views of Jumbo Pass, as well as Redtop Mountain and the Sunday Glacier.

Access:
From Panorama drive west on the Toby Creek FSR. Stay on the main road. At 19 km the road turns right up the Jumbo valley and becomes the Jumbo FSR. Continue on this road for another 3km. Just as you come into an open area where a large avalanche path reaches the road on the left, look for a somewhat grown in ATV track on the right. Park here.

Trail:
Follow the ATV track. Initially it is a bit rough but it soon improves. It skirts around the edges of an avalanche path before going back into the forest. At 1.75 km it switchbacks to the right and after 300 m it switchbacks left again. At this point the track becomes fairly steep. After another 500 m a narrower trail goes around a washout. If you look across the valley here you will get a good view of Jumbo Pass, and even the Cauldron Glacier beyond. For the next couple kilometers, the trail is a bit overgrown however the bed surface is quite good. At 4.6 kilometers cross a creek. Shortly after, the trail switchbacks a couple times, gaining elevation beside a large avalanche path. The views of the valley start to open up here. At 5.5 kilometers there is a junction. Go straight, towards the head of the valley rather than turning right. The trail drops down slightly before climbing up again, along a section where

rockfall has narrowed the trail. Continue climbing. A couple short switchbacks help you gain elevation quickly. The old road continues into the

alpine. Eventually it peters out. At this point you could climb to the pass above you on the right for views into the Delphine Valley.

Alternatively, continue straight ahead to the pass at the head of the valley for views of the Farnham valley and the Cleaver beyond.

Option:

From the pass at the head of the valley, it is possible to climb to a peak which overlooks the Farnham Glacier. It is another 2 kilometers from the pass via fairly straightforward ridge walking. It is a truly spectacular spot, with peaks and glaciers in all directions.

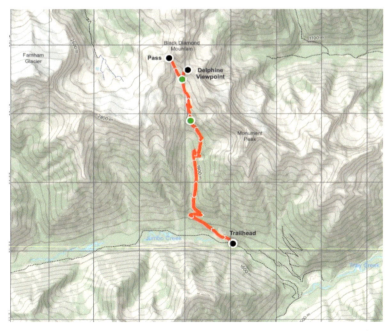

32 Jumbo Pass

Distance: 8 km
Time: 3-4 hours
Elevation Gain: 712 m

Jumbo Pass is a very popular hike and for good reason. For a small amount of effort, you get to experience sublime alpine meadows with views of glaciers and peaks. The decades-long battle over a proposed ski resort in this valley came to a conclusion in 2019 when the resort idea was finally put to rest. In January 2020 it was announced that the Jumbo Valley will be turned into an Indigenous Protected and Conserved Area as it holds high spiritual and cultural significance for the Ktunaxa people who call this area Qat'muk.

Jumbo Pass. Photo: Cam Mclellan

Access:
From Panorama drive west on the Toby Creek FSR. Stay on the main road. At 19 km the road turns right up the Jumbo valley and becomes the Jumbo FSR. Continue on this road for another 15.4 km. The last few kilometers are quite rough and you have to drive through a small creek.

Trail:

From the trailhead you head up an overgrown old road bed for a hundred metres before the trail turns uphill into the forest. It climbs steadily through lush mature timber. Eventually the trail emerges into subalpine meadows continuing to climb to the pass. In mid summer the meadows are carpeted with wild flowers and in fall the larches glow yellow. After you reach a high point the trail drops into a notch. Here is the junction with the trail from the Glacier Creek valley accessed from Argenta in the West Kootenays. A helpful sign points to east and west. It would be very inconvenient to take the wrong trail and end up hundreds of kilometers from your vehicle. From the junction the trail climbs out of the notch and along the height of the pass. The Jumbo Pass cabin sits near the north end of the pass below an unnamed peak. It can be booked through the Columbia Valley Hut Society. If the hut is booked, or if you prefer to camp, there are camp spots near the tarn below the hut. Please take care of the fragile alpine meadows by staying on existing trails and using existing camp spots.

Ridgewalk above Jumbo Pass Cabin. Photo: Cam Mclellan

Options:

From the hut a faint steep trail leads up to the unnamed peak behind the hut. The views of the Cauldron glacier and the Macbeth Icefield to the west and Jumbo Mountain and Karnak to the east cannot be beat and the views improve the higher up on the ridge you get. 30 minutes to the first bump. From Jumbo Pass you can also scramble Bastille Mountain (see hike #33)

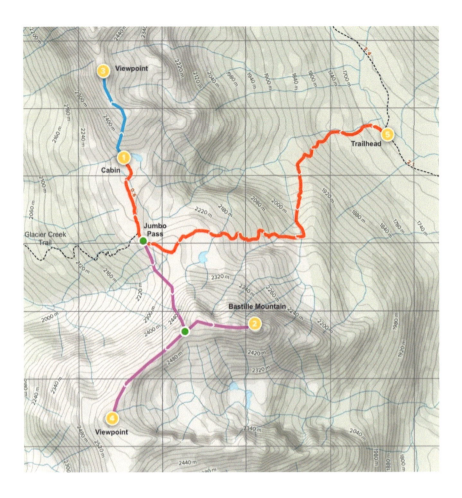

33 Bastille Mountain (scramble)

Distance: 4 km (from Jumbo Pass)
Time: 2-3 hours
Elevation Gain: 300 m

Bastille Mountain is the prominent peak with four summits which flanks the south end of Jumbo Pass. Even though it is only a short climb from the popular Jumbo Pass hike it does not see many ascents. To get to the first summit is relatively easy, only requiring comfort with loose scree and talus. To gain the main summit you have to climb over the other three peaks. It is never difficult but does involve some loose rock, route finding and exposure. It is a highly enjoyable climb and the rock gets better the further along you go. The panorama from the top includes incredible views of the highest peaks in the Purcells and the glaciers and peaks of the Cauldron group.

Access:
See Jumbo Pass hike #32.

Route:
From Jumbo Pass head south along the height of land to the base of Bastille Mountain. Follow a faint goat trail into the scree gully visible from the pass. Scramble up this loose scree gully, with better footing to climbers right. At the top of the gully look for a faint trail to the left which leads to another short gully with loose rock. From the top of this gully it is an easy ridge walk to the first summit. From the first summit descend slightly down and right, then at the base of the next peak climb up on loose downsloping slabs to a notch right at the ridge top. A few exposed but easy moves on relatively solid rock lead to the next peak. Descend the far side and cross the grassy slope to the next peak. One or two easy moves on solid rock gain a ledge system which leads to the next peak. The rock is now solid blocky quartzite. Traverse along the ridge to the final peak. Traverse on a low ledge system until right below the summit then climb up to the summit on good rock. Descend the same way. You can also continue west from the top of the scree gully and continue easily along ridgelines for another kilometer. From here the views of the Cauldron glacier to the west are fantastic.

HORSETHIEF CREEK

34 Mount Bruce

Distance: 6.4 km
Time: 3 hours
Elevation Gain: 664 m

Mount Bruce Summit Plateau

Mount Bruce is the fairly nondescript rounded mountain just west of Invermere but don't be fooled by its appearance. It is a short hike to a lovely alpine plateau with fantastic views of the Columbia Valley and the high mountains to the west.

Access:
From Invermere drive to Wilmer. Turn left on Park Street in Wilmer which turns into Horsethief FSR. Continue on this for 18 km until you reach Ryan Creek Main on the left. If you miss it and keep going straight the road will deteriorate fairly quickly. Turn left on Ryan Creek Main and start driving up the backside of Mount Bruce. There are a few small water bars but high clearance is not needed. The trailhead is at the end of the road on a landing. Look for a flagged trail at the end of the landing.

Trail:

To begin with the trail climbs quite steeply through a cutblock of replanted trees. It then goes into the forest and crosses a tiny stream with a log carved into a water pipe. This is the last access to water on the hike. The trail climbs through talus and forest, eventually emerging onto the broad summit plateau. There is some flagging and a cairn to mark the trail. Make note of this spot so you can find the trail again on your way back. From here continue to meander along the plateau to the far end. A small cairn marks the summit. Just downhill from the summit is a good sheltered lunch spot which overlooks the Panorama ski resort. Return the way you came.

35 Redline Peak (scramble)

Distance: 14 km (depending on how far you can drive)
Time: 5-7 hours
Elevation Gain: 1200 m

Redline Peak is a glaciated peak at the head of McDonald Creek. It is surrounded by some of the highest peaks in the Purcells and has great views. The direct route up the glacier requires glacier travel and crevasse rescue skills however the route described here only requires some moderate scrambling. There are also old mine shafts and relics in the area. Do not enter any mine shafts as they may be unstable. The Red Line Mine has an interesting history. According to "Mines in the Windermere Valley" by the Windermere Valley Museum and Archives, "A group of Eastern American investors [...] used the property to supply silver to their jewelry store, Tiffany's in New York City" in the early 1900s.

Summit of Redline Peak in spring

Access:
From Radium drive west on the Horsethief FSR which begins just past the Canfor mill. At km 9 there is a four-way intersection. Go straight through the intersection towards Lake of the Hanging Glacier. At km 13 there is another intersection by a gravel pit. Stay left (right goes to Forster Creek). Continue on the Horsethief FSR

until km 33. Turn left on McDonald Creek and start climbing out of the valley. The road is quite rough and requires 4WD and high clearance. Depending on the state of the road and your comfort with driving on rough roads you may be able to drive to the basin below Redline Peak, or you may have to walk the last few km.

Route:

Once you reach the basin below the glacier, continue on the rough road which goes left and climbs up into a valley to the east. You will see some old mine shafts and remnants of an old cabin. Once in this valley turn south and start climbing up the talus, eventually gaining the rocky ridge which leads to the first summit. Drop down to a small pass and cross over to the main summit, scrambling up on easy terrain. The summit is marked with a large cairn and a wooden plaque. Return the same way.

36 Commander Glacier

Distance: 4.5 km
Time: 2-3 hours
Elevation Gain: 350 m

This hike follows the crest of an old moraine to a rocky plateau below the impressive Commander Glacier. Do not venture onto the glacier unless you have the skills and equipment.

Commander Glacier. The trail follows the moraine at bottom left.
Peaks L to R: The Cleaver, the Three Guardsmen, Commander Mountain.

Access:
From Radium drive west on the Horsethief FSR which begins just past the Canfor mill. At km 9 there is a four-way intersection. Go straight through the intersection towards Lake of the Hanging Glacier. At km 13 there is another intersection by a gravel pit. Stay left (right goes to Forster Creek). Continue on the Horsethief FSR until km 41.5 then turn left to go up the Farnham Valley (right goes to Lake of the Hanging Glacier). Continue up this road for another 12.1 km. The road will go downhill slightly until you come to a large landing across from the Commander Glacier. Past this landing the road gets much rougher and starts climbing again. Park in the landing.

Trail:
Look for a small cairn at the edge of landing. If you can't find the cairn just look over the edge and look for a small trail going downhill between the fireweed. This trail crosses an old ATV track very shortly. Continue to follow

this fairly well marked trail until you reach the creek. Cross on some logs and continue in the forest for a few hundred meters until the trail starts climbing. Eventually the trail gains the crest of the moraine, in spots dropping left below the crest where trees block the way or where the moraine has eroded. Be careful with your footing on the moraine. Do not climb all the way to the end of the moraine but rather when you are 100 m or so before some cliffs look for a faint marked trail going downhill across to some rock slabs. Continue to follow this faint trail and climb up the rock slabs until you gain the crest of the rocky plateau below the glacier.

Options:

You can scramble up left to a waterfall coming off the glacier. Or continue across the plateau, being very careful crossing the creeks coming off the glacier. The water moves fast and the rocks are slippery.

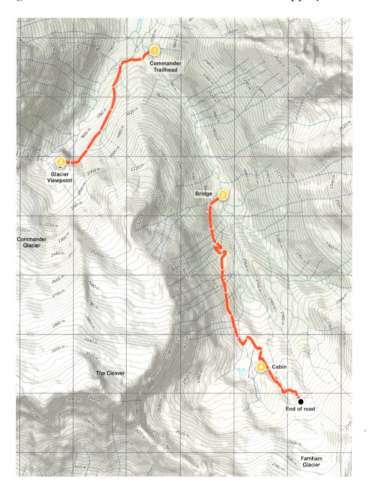

37 Farnham Glacier

Distance: 8 km
Time: 3-4 hours
Elevation Gain: 220 m

The Farnham Glacier was once the site of the Canadian ski team summer training camp. It was also at the center of the debate about the Jumbo ski resort. It is hard to imagine now but big trucks with supplies used to drive right up to the glacier. If you are an adventurous driver and have a 4WD with high clearance or an ATV you may still be able to drive right to the ice. Most people now park at the last bridge, which continues to deteriorate, and walk up the road. There is a user maintained cabin near the toe of the glacier. It is first come first serve.

Farnham Glacier in late fall.

Access:

From Radium drive west on the Horsethief FSR which begins just past the Canfor mill. At km 9 there is a four way intersection. Go straight through the intersection towards Lake of the Hanging Glacier. At km 13 there is another intersection by a gravel pit. Stay left (right goes to Forster Creek). Continue on the Horsethief FSR until km 41.5 then turn left to go up the Farnham Valley (right goes to Lake of the Hanging Glacier). Bridge 11.4 k Continue up this road, for another 14.4 km, until a deteriorating bridge before a big climb up the left side of the valley. Park here. The last couple kilometers require 4WD and high clearance.

Toe of the Farnham Glacier

Trail:
Walk up the old road. It switchbacks a couple times before the terrain levels out and the road goes below some big slopes. Cross the creek and pass the cabin. Continue on the rough road until you reach the glacier. Do not venture onto the ice unless you have the necessary skills and training.

Options:
The ridges and basins around Farnham Glacier lend themselves to off trail ramblings and exploration.

38 Lake of the Hanging Glacier

Distance: 16 km
Time: 6-8 hours
Elevation Gain: 947 m

Lake of the Hanging Glacier

This is a very popular trail, and for very good reason. It is both about the journey and the destination. The trail goes from valley bottom poplar groves, past waterfalls to alpine meadows and finishes at a turquoise lake ringed with spectacular glacier covered peaks. There are often icebergs floating in the lake. It does not get much better than this!

Please note: the Summit Trail Makers Society removes the bridge over Hellroaring creek each fall and replaces it in early summer. Check http://www.summittrailmakers.ca/lake-of-hanging-glacier.html for the status of the bridge. The creek crossing would be very dangerous and difficult without the bridge in place.

Access:
From Radium drive west past the Canfor sawmill on the Horsethief Creek FSR. At the 4 way intersection at KM 9 go straight (it is well signed) and

continue on the Horsethief FSR. At another intersection at KM 13 stay left. Continue on this road until KM 41.5. Stay right here. The road goes downhill and crosses Horsethief creek. Be sure to stop and check out the impressive slot canyon just below the bridge! The road continues another 8 km from the junction and ends at the trailhead. The last few km are quite rough and have had several washouts in the past. A high clearance vehicle is needed for the last 6 km.

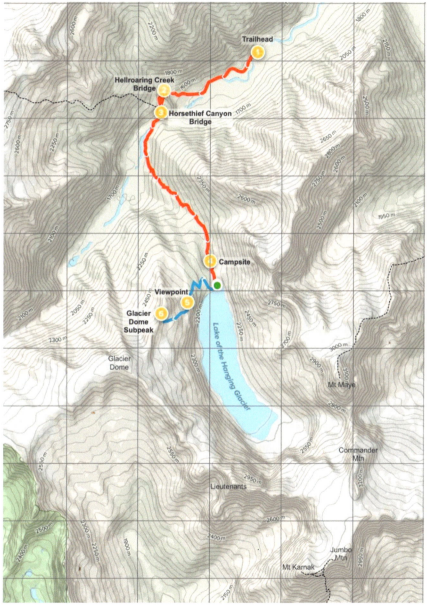

Trail:
Follow an old road bed for 2 km through pleasant open poplar and coniferous forest. The trail then narrows and climbs up before crossing the footbridge over Hell Roaring Creek. Descend slightly to a second bridge, over Horsethief Creek. Continue through mature forest and then start climbing at a moderate grade, via many switchbacks. This part of the hike is very pleasant as it goes along a series of cascading waterfalls, with many spots to stop and enjoy the cooling spray from the creek. Once the terrain levels out again the trail enters alpine meadows. About 700 m before the lake there is a small campsite with a toilet and picnic tables. Camping at the lake is not recommended as it gets very windy, and the meadows are quite fragile.

Options:
From the lake it is possible to scramble Glacier Dome Subpeak. See hike #39.

For a less committing option, hike up to the ridge just west of the lake's outflow for spectacular views of the lake and the glacier at the far end of the lake. See the Glacier Dome Subpeak description.

39 Glacier Dome Subpeak (scramble)

Distance: 4 km (from Lake of the Hanging Glaciers)
Time: 3 hours
Elevation Gain: 400 m

This easy scramble starts at Lake of the Hanging Glaciers. It leads to a high point on the northeast ridge of Glacier Dome from where you get spectacular views of the lake, Starbird Pass to the west and the glaciated peaks to the north. To climb Glacier Dome itself requires crossing a glacier with sizeable crevasses and is not recommended unless you have the necessary equipment and skills.

Access:
See Lake of the Hanging Glaciers.

Route:
Cross the outflow of the lake on flat rocks. On the far side a faint trail climbs up and right into the trees. Follow this trail as it gains elevation. There are cairns to mark the route though at times it is hard to follow. In general, the route goes up and left, circumventing small cliff bands where necessary. Once you gain the sparsely treed rocky ridge at treeline follow it to its far south end. It is about an hour to this point from where you get spectacular views of the lake and the glaciers at its far end. Turn around here if you are looking for the shorter option. To continue to the top, continue up the talus field to a flat spot on the ridge above. While tempting to go straight up from here to the summit, the direct way is fairly loose and steep. It is better to cross into the bowl on the other side and diagonal up and right to the subpeak which is marked by a cairn. About 1.5-2 hours. Return the way you came.

FORSTER CREEK

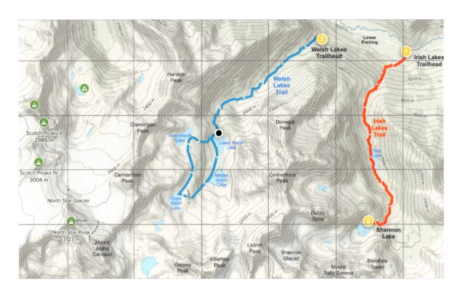

40 Irish Lakes

Distance: 12 km
Time: 4-5 hours
Elevation Gain: 830 m

The Irish Lakes are not as well known as the nearby Welsh Lakes. The trail is rough and steep, though well marked. In 2017 a piece of the Shannon Glacier fell off and triggered a tsunami, which wiped out a good part of the

old trail. You can still see evidence of this event when you travel up the canyon as there are many downed trees in the creek bed. The trail has recently been rebuilt. Do not attempt this hike when water levels are high as you have to cross Irish Creek on some slippery logs, which would be dangerous in high water conditions. There is some route finding required to get to Shannon Lake.

Access:
From Radium drive west on the Horsethief FSR which begins just past the Canfor mill. At KM 9 there is a four way intersection. Go straight through. At KM 13 there is another intersection by a gravel pit. Go right, to Forster Creek. Continue on the Forster FSR until KM 35.3 where the road crosses Irish Creek. Park just before the bridge in a wide spot.

Trail:
The trail begins just before the bridge on the uphill side of the road. It initially winds through a mossy forest and then climbs up to meet Irish Creek. Follow the left bank for a few hundred meters until you see the well flagged crossing spot. Continue to climb steeply on the far side. Once the terrain levels out a bit you cross several talus slopes, reaching Tara Lake after 3.5 km. Continue on the right side of Tara Lake, boulder hopping, to the far end. Cross on boulders and then start climbing up through the forest again. The trail climbs above an impressive canyon before becoming less distinct in the talus above. You will reach an open boulder field with the creek just in front of you. It is easiest to walk up the rock slabs next to the creek, passing several beautiful waterfalls on your way to Shannon Lake, which is a lovely lake set in a rocky basin, with granite peaks towering above.

Tara Lake

41 Welsh Lakes

Distance: 8+ km
Time: 3-4 hours
Elevation Gain: 550 m

The Welsh Lakes are four subalpine turquoise lakes in a spectacular setting. In the summer there are legions of wildflowers and in the fall the valley is filled with larches. Bonus points if you can pronounce Aberystwyth Lake, which requires some off trail hiking to get to.

Welsh Lakes. Photo: Austin Stone

Access:
From Radium drive west on the Horsethief FSR which begins just past the Canfor mill. At KM 9 there is a four way intersection. Go straight. At KM 13 there is another intersection by a gravel pit. Go right, to Forster Creek. Continue on the Forster FSR until km 36 then turn left towards Welsh Lakes. The last 1.8 km requires 4WD and high clearance or you can park at km 36 and walk up the last road. In the last couple of years the Forster FSR has become very rutted, which may require a higher clearance vehicle though this may change.

Trail:

From the parking lot the trail goes straight ahead and then crosses the creek. It goes through the forest for the first couple kilometers until you are in a basin below a headwall. The trail climbs to the right of the headwall, above a canyon and eventually reaches the first lake.

Middle Welsh Lake. Photo: AJ McGrath

Options:

From lower Welsh Lake you can climb the slopes to the right to reach Aberystwyth Lake or continue straight ahead for middle and upper Welsh Lakes. A nice off trail loop goes up to Aberystwyth, gaining 150m through open forest, then traverses across a plateau to Upper Welsh Lake and drops back down, following the creek to Middle Welsh Lake, where the trail picks up again.

It is also possible to continue past Upper Welsh Lake through talus and moraines to a pass at the head of the valley, between Alpha Centauri and Galway Peak. This is a truly stunning spot overlooking the Horsethief Valley and the peaks to the south.

42 Olive Hut/Catamount Glacier

Distance: 15 km
Time: 5-7 hours
Elevation Gain: 945 m

The Olive Hut is a stone cabin set on a granite ridge overlooking the Catamount Glacier. It is necessary to cross the glacier to reach the cabin. While the Catamount Glacier is fairly benign, you should have glacier travel skills and equipment. The hut sleeps 4 comfortably and can be booked through the Columbia Valley Hut Society. It was built by the Olive Family in 1991 to commemorate siblings Peter and Brenda, who died in helicopter accidents.

Access:
From Radium drive west on the Horsethief FSR which begins just past the Canfor mill. At km 9 there is a four-way intersection. Go straight through the intersection, towards Lake of the Hanging Glacier. At km 13 there is another intersection by a gravel pit. Go right, to Forster Creek. Continue on the Forster FSR until the end, at KM 42. The last few kilometers of the Forster FSR are very rough and 4WD and high clearance is recommended.

Catamount Glacier. Photo: Ian Houghton

Trail:
Cross the creek on a wooden bridge and start climbing up the hillside on a rough old road. Where the road curves left, a steep shortcut trail goes straight up and rejoins the road. After the road crests it descends to the marshy Forster Creek Basin. On the left is the Snowmobile Society warming cabin. Once in the Forster basin the road angles left. A flagged trail leads into the trees and eventually crosses the creek on some logs. The trail becomes less

distinct but eventually comes out into a wide fan shaped moraine. You want to climb to the top of this slope. The trail gets indistinct as you climb up. Once the angle eases off you go into a little gully flanked by a steep cliff on the left. Continue around this cliff, climbing up a short steep slope and entering a bowl with the toe of the glacier at the end of it. If you are not prepared to venture onto the glacier turn around here. Otherwise, start up the fairly mellow toe of the glacier and continue going uphill until you reach the flats of the Catamount Glacier. The Olive Hut is located on the second rock rib on the left and is invisible from below as it blends into the rocks. The easiest way to reach the hut is to go into the basin below Scotch Peaks and traverse up and left on low angled benches to gain the hut.

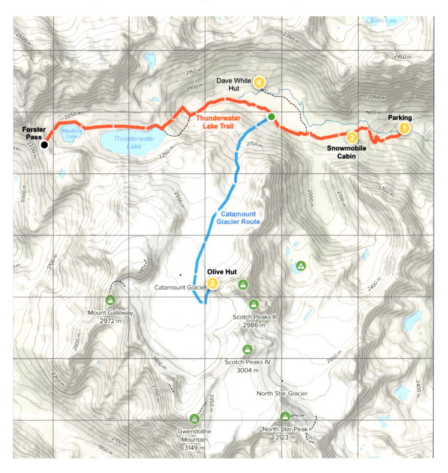

43 Thunderwater Lake

Distance: 14 km
Time: 5-7 hours
Elevation Gain: 455 m

Thunderwater Lake is a high alpine turquoise lake in a spectacular setting. The approach is challenging, as it requires good route finding skills. It is likely your feet will get wet as you have to travel through boggy sections and there are several creek crossings.

Access:
From Radium drive west on the Horsethief FSR which begins just past the Canfor mill. At km 9 there is a four way intersection. Go straight through the intersection towards Lake of the Hanging Glacier. At km 13 there is another intersection by a gravel pit. Go right, to Forster Creek. Continue on the Forster FSR until the end, at KM 42. In the last couple of years the Forster FSR has become very rutted which may require more clearance than usual. This will likely change year to year.

Trail:
Cross the creek on a wooden bridge and start climbing up the hillside on a rough old road. Where the road curves left, a steep shortcut trail goes straight up and rejoins the road. After the road crests it descends to the marshy Forster Creek Basin. On the left is the Snowmobile Society warming cabin. Once in the Forster basin the road angles left. A flagged trail leads into the trees and eventually crosses the creek on some logs. The trail becomes less distinct but eventually comes out into a wide fan shaped moraine. Cross the moraine, and the creek which flows out from Catamount Glacier. Look for bits of flagging though the trail is quite indistinct through the marshes. As you near the headwall below Thunderwater Lake cross the creek to the other side of the basin and start up rock slabs which angle up and left. Once you crest the headwall the lake is just a short distance ahead. There are some nice spots to camp, though no facilities.

Options:
You can contour around the lake and continue to Whirlpool Lake above. From Whirlpool Lake it is a short climb to Forster Pass, from which you get great views to the West Kootenays.

Thunderwater Lake in July

FRANCES CREEK

44 Buster (Azure) Lake

Distance: 10.5 km
Time: 3-4 hours
Elevation Gain: 767 m

This popular hike leads to two alpine lakes which are a tropical shade of blue. The trailhead is the same as Mclean Lake and the two hikes can be combined via a fantastic ridgeline scramble.

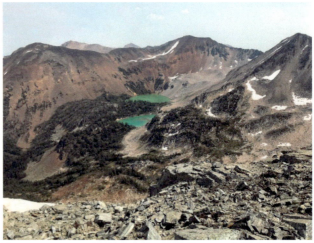

Access:
From Invermere drive to Wilmer. Past Wilmer the road turns to West Side Road. Go north on this road to 41.5 km. You may see the green RSTBC sign for McLean Lake Trail. Turn west onto the Lead Queen Mine road. Take the left branch at the junction, this is the Francis Creek FSR. Follow this road to the trailhead, about 15 km from Westside Road. Stay left at any junctions and follow signage for McLean Lake Trail.

Trail:
Follow the trail from the trailhead sign a short distance to the first creek crossing where there is a log and cable bridge across Francis Creek. At 2.2 km the trail reaches the second creek crossing, the outflow creek from Buster Lake where there is a log and cable bridge. At approximately 4 km you leave the forest to cross a scree slope, then pass a small pond to reach a steep headwall. Follow the switchback trail up the headwall. After the headwall the trail climbs consistently up through meadows to reach the upper lake at about 5 km. Follow the path around the lake to the right for about 500 m. From here you can follow the outflow creek to the lower lake, though there is no trail.

Option:

The traverse between Buster and Mclean Lakes is a fantastic ridgeline scramble, high above the Forster and Frances Creek drainages with stellar views of the Catamount Glacier. Start at Buster Lake. Traverse around the lower lake and continue up to a pass, going through boulders and talus. From the pass head up the ridge on the right. It is not as difficult as it looks from below. Scramble up and continue along the ridge. At a steeper spot traverse left around a small drop off. Eventually the ridge becomes grassier. Drop down to the pass at the end of the ridge from which you can see McLean Lake. Continue downhill towards McLean Lake, and start traversing left towards a tiny tarn. Climb the ridge behind the tarn, then traverse to the right, reaching McLean Lake. Continue to the outflow of McLean Lake where you pick up the trail.

On the ridge between Buster and McLean Lakes, looking towards Catamount Glacier and Thunderwater Lake.

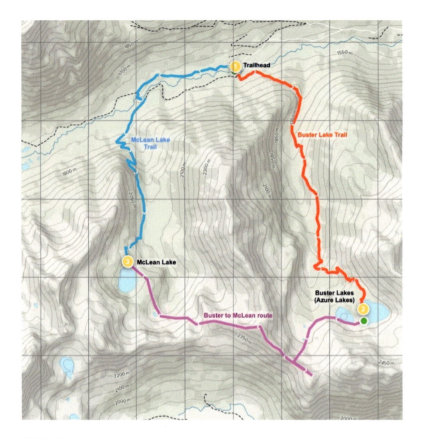

45 McLean Lake

Distance: 11.4 km
Time: 3-4 hours
Elevation Gain: 575 m

McLean Lake is a beautiful blue lake located in a high elevation basin at the headwaters of McLean Creek. The area was once busy with mining. In the early and mid 1900s packhorses were used to drag ore down from the Leadqueen Mine across the valley. The trails can still be seen to the north across the Frances Creek valley from the McLean Lake Trail. The mine on McLean Creek was active as late as 1980.

Access:
From Invermere drive to Wilmer. Past Wilmer the road turns to West Side Road. Go north on this road to 41.5 km. You may see the green RSTBC sign for McLean Lake Trail. Turn west onto the Lead Queen Mine road. Take the left branch at the junction, this is the Francis Creek FSR. Follow this road to

the trailhead, about 15 km from Westside Road. Stay left at any junctions and follow signage for McLean Lake Trail.

McLean Lake. Photo: Taoya Schaefer

Trail:
The trail initially goes through the forest, skirting recent cutblocks for almost 2 km. Stay left at a fork. The right goes to Septet Pass. After crossing the bridge over Frances Creek, you reach an old road. Continue on the old road and a little further up there is another creek crossing, consisting of a couple of logs. Continue for another 2 km, switchbacking through the forest high above McLean Creek. Eventually you cross rubble fields. A side trail at about 4.5 km goes to a viewpoint overlooking a waterfall. Back on the main trail, you re-enter the forest and continue climbing until the terrain finally levels out. In mid summer the meadows are carpeted with wildflowers. The trail ends at McLean Lake. There is a small campsite by the lake.

Options:
For the traverse between McLean and Buster Lakes see hike #44. Scrambling up to the pass southeast of the lake is also worthwhile for the amazing views of the Catamount Glacier immediately to the south.

Photo: Taoya Schaefer

46 Septet Pass

Distance: 19 km
Time: 5-7 hours
Elevation Gain: 620 m

Septet Pass is a beautiful alpine area which is several kilometers long. Chalice Ridge (hike #55) is just to the west, and it can be reached from Septet Pass

as well. Septet Pass can be hiked either from the Frances Creek or the Bugaboo Creek side. It is a great area for exploring alpine meadows carpeted with wildflowers

Septet Pass. Photo: Alex Geary

Access

The Frances Creek trailhead is the same as the McLean Lake trailhead. To reach it, drive from Invermere to Wilmer. Past Wilmer the road turns to West Side Road. Go north on this road to 41.5 km. You may see the green RSTBC sign for McLean Lake Trail. Turn left onto the Lead Queen Mine road. After 1.6 km turn left on the Francis Creek FSR. Follow this road to the trailhead at Km 17.5. Park near the old bridge over Frances Creek.

For access from Bugaboo Creek, drive north from Radium to Brisco. Turn left on Brisco Road and cross the multiple channels of the Columbia River. Continue past Patty's Greenhouse and a small gravel pit and turn left at KM 5. Go uphill. At KM 7 turn right on Bugaboo FSR - the kilometers reset to 0 here. Stay right at Km 11.5, following the signs for CMH. Turn left at KM 36.9, the right goes to Bugaboo Provincial Park. Stay left at the next intersection and cross Bugaboo Creek. After crossing the creek go left to Septet Creek.

Septet Pass. Photo: Alex Geary

Trail:
From Frances Creek, follow the McLean Lake trail for about 1.6 km, along the north side of the creek. Where the trail forks, stay right. Continue up the valley through open avalanche paths. After 2.5 km start climbing more steeply in mature forest as you leave the Frances Creek valley. Cross a small creek, and the trail levels out again. As the terrain opens up and you enter the pass, the trail is less distinct. Make note of where the trail starts for the return trip. Cairns mark the trail in the alpine.

Options:
A faint trail connects Septet Pass to Chalice Ridge (hike #55). Or else, continue through the pass to Septet Creek on the other side. From the pass it is 8 km to the trailhead on the Bugaboo side. The alpine basin to the east is also worthwhile. Travel off trail through open forest to gain the bench which is nestled below the craggy peaks of the Septet Range. There are several small tarns.

Septet Pass. Photo: Alex Geary

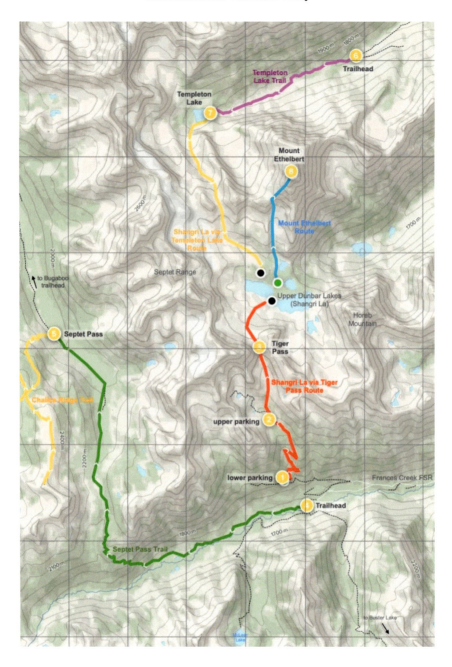

47 Shangri La via Tiger Pass

Distance: 12 km
Time: 4-5 hours
Elevation Gain: 1200 m

Shangri La (Upper Dunbar Lakes) is a splendid area with lakes in different shades of turquoise. There are oodles of wildflowers and larches, and the basin is surrounded by the rugged peaks of the Septet Range. To access Shangri La via Tiger Pass requires crossing a small pocket glacier which does have some crevasses. Alternatively, it can be reached via an off trail route from Templeton Lake. Tiger Pass itself is a worthwhile destination as you get fantastic views of peaks, lakes, and glaciers. The road to the pass was built for mining operations and there are still mining relics all over the place.

One of the many turquoise lakes at Shangri La with Mount Horeb in the background

Access:
Drive from Invermere through Wilmer. Past Wilmer the road turns to West Side Road. Go north on this road to 41.5 km. You may see a sign for McLean Lake Trail. Turn left onto the Lead Queen Mine road. After 1.6 km turn left on the Francis Creek FSR. Follow this road to the trailhead for 15.7 km. A

road goes right, uphill here. Most drivers will likely want to park here and walk the 4.4 km up the old road. If you have nerves of steel and enjoy hairpin corners requiring 3 point turns, steep drop offs, and washed out road surfaces - carry on!

Trail:
Walk up the road until you reach a creek crossing. The road continues beyond the creek but the trail goes up a steep forested slope before the creek, towards Tiger Pass. Once the terrain levels out, you leave the forest behind and continue through open slopes and flowery meadows towards the pass. The trail becomes indistinct as you approach the pass. Looking south you get a fantastic view across the Frances Creek valley towards the Catamount Glacier. One the north side of Tiger Pass you get the first glimpses into the Shangri La basin. It is strongly recommended to have crevasse rescue equipment, even though the glacier is quite small. You may also want microspikes or crampons for traction. The route down to the left is generally less crevassed. Once you reach the end of the glacier continue through scree fields to the lakes. There are many great places to camp. There are no facilities and please follow leave no trace practices to keep this beautiful area pristine.

Looking across at the pocket glacier at Tiger Pass

Options:
If you have two vehicles, you could hike out via Templeton Lake, see hike #49 for description. A scramble up mount Ethelbert (see hike #48) is very worthwhile. Or else, explore the basin, going up the pass towards Templeton Lake and exploring the different lakes.

48 Mount Ethelbert 3175 m

Distance: 3 km (from Shangri La)
Time: 3-4 hours
Elevation Gain: 960 m

The high peak just north of the Shangri La area was named for Sister Ethelbert, a nun who died in 1886 on a riverboat while traveling the Columbia River. The peak is visible from the Columbia Valley, and an interpretive sign on the highway just north of Brisco tells the story of the unfortunate nun. Mount Ethelbert is a fairly straightforward scramble and the views from the summit are outstanding, including views of the Bugaboos and the Catamount Glacier.

Access:
Via the Shangri La basin, which can be accessed either via Tiger Pass (hike #47) or Templeton Lake (hike #49)

Route:
From the Shangri La basin, head towards the obvious scree cone at the base of Mount Ethelbert. Start climbing up the scree cone, which may be somewhat tedious. Once on top of the scree cone, go left towards a lower angle ridge on the southwest side of the peak. Continue up this ridge, which is easy and blocky, to reach the summit.

Scrambling route on Mount Ethelbert

BUGABOO CREEK

49 Templeton Lake

Distance: 9.4 km
Time: 4 hours
Elevation Gain: 280 m
Map Page 112

Templeton Lake is a surreal shade of turquoise. It is fed by a hanging glacier which clings to the rugged peaks of the Septet Range circling this gorgeous lake. The hike is not long, nor is it overly strenuous. Templeton Lake can also be used to access Shangri-La via a fairly straightforward overland route.

Access:
From Radium, drive north towards Brisco. Turn left on Brisco Road and cross the multiple channels of the Columbia River. Continue past Patty's Greenhouse and a small gravel pit and turn left at KM 5. Go uphill. At KM 7 turn right on Bugaboo FSR. Continue for 11.5km and turn left, towards Cartwright Lake. The right goes towards the Bugaboos. The kilometer markers now start counting down from 57. Go for about 4 km, and turn right on Templeton Main, just after the 54 km marker. After 3.2 km take the road which goes left, and starts climbing up through a cutblock. Continue another 6 km. Park where the road curves left. The trail is where the old roadbed goes straight.

Trail:
Follow the old roadbed and cross the creek on a decent bridge. Continue through the forest for a couple kilometers until you reach a large talus slope. The trail makes a sharp left here and crosses to the other side of the creek, though the creek goes underground here. On the other side of the creek follow cairns along the edge of the talus. After a few hundred meters you come to a beautiful blue pool, and some marshlands with small beaver dams. The trail is less distinct through the talus. Once you reach the end of the talus the trail veers sharply right again and goes into the trees. The final climb to the lake is steeper but the trail remains fairly obvious. There are several great lunch spots along the lake shore and there is one small flat spot to camp if you continue left around the lake for 50 meters. Otherwise camp spots are pretty limited.

Options:
From Templeton Lake it is a fairly straightforward route to Shangri La which avoids the glacier crossing on the Tiger Pass route. It is also worthwhile to

just climb up to the pass which overlooks Shangri La, which can be done as a day hike. Either way, continue clockwise around the lake on a fairly obvious trail. When you reach a talus slope after about 400 m start going uphill. A faint trail climbs steeply up the gully. Once the angle eases off continue uphill on moraines. The going is less steep and the route becomes quite obvious though there is no trail. Continue up this moraine covered valley until you reach the height of land which separates Shangri La from Templeton Lake, about 1.5 - 2 h from Templeton Lake. You can look across at Tiger Pass and see the small pocket glacier. You can also see the different colored lakes of Shangri La. Turn around here or continue down the far side to Shangri La, which is another 2.5 km away from the pass, via undulating moraines.

The turquoise waters of Templeton Lake

50 Rocky Point

Distance: 17 km
Time: 6-7 hours
Elevation Gain: 1050 m

This area is popular with snowmobilers in the winter. In the summer it is a non-motorized trail. It leads to alpine meadows and ridges with great views of the Bugaboos to the west. In the summer the meadows are filled with wildflowers and in the fall the larches are golden.

View of the Vowell Glacier from Rockypoint ridge.
Photo: Andrew McLeod

Access:
From Radium, drive north towards Brisco. Turn left on Brisco Road and cross the multiple channels of the Columbia River. Continue past Patty's Greenhouse and a small gravel pit and turn left at KM 5. Go uphill. At KM 7 turn right on Bugaboo FSR. The kilometer markers reset to 0 here. Stay right at KM 11.5, following the signs for CMH. Park at KM 29.5 by a trail kiosk.

Trail:

Follow the wide trail as it switchbacks up the hill. Eventually it levels out and continues up the valley, crossing several large avalanche paths. The trail is boggy in places. After the trail skirts a talus slope it drops down slightly. Here the trail narrows, after it crosses a small creek. It climbs up more steeply and then emerges into open meadows. Pass remnants of old cabins. Continue all the way up to the ridge from where you have panoramic views of the Bugaboos and the Vowell glacier.

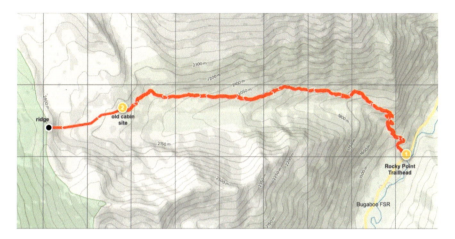

Options:

It is possible to traverse from Rockypoint basin to Cobalt Lake. Follow faint trails on the backside of Rockypoint ridge or stay on the ridge itself.

51 Cobalt Lake

Distance: 15.1 km
Time: 5-7 hours
Elevation Gain: 1216 m

Cobalt Lake is tucked into an alpine basin ringed by Cobalt Spire, Brenta Spire and Northpost Spire. The famous Northeast ridge of Bugaboo Spire is visible directly above the lake. It is a fantastic alpine environment.

Please note - Cobalt Lake is in Bugaboo Provincial Park where dogs are not allowed.

Cobalt Lake. Photo: AJ McGrath

Access:
From Radium, drive north towards Brisco. Turn left on Brisco Road and cross the multiple channels of the Columbia River. Continue past Patty's Greenhouse and a small gravel pit and turn left at KM 5. Go uphill. At KM 7 turn right on Bugaboo FSR. The kilometer markers reset to 0 here. Stay right at Km 11.5, following the signs for CMH. Turn right at 36.9 km onto a rougher, narrower road. The Cobalt Lake trailhead is about 1.5 km down this road on the right.

Trail:

The trail begins along the park access road directly across from the CMH lodge. Begin by climbing a series of steep switchbacks up an old skid road. At 3.2 km there is a junction. The main trail goes right while a short side trail goes to Walter Lake on the left. After another kilometer on the main trail, you reach a pass. From the pass go up the open alpine ridge to the right from where you have good views of Cobalt Lake and the Bugaboo Spires. To reach the lake, continue along to the end of the ridge, then descend to an alpine pass and contour under Northpost Spire to below the waterfalls draining Cobalt Lake. Bypass the waterfalls on the left to gain the meadows surrounding the lake. The last 2 km to the lake requires route finding skills as the trail is not well marked.

Options:

It is possible to traverse from Cobalt Lake to the Conrad Kain Hut via an alpine route which crosses talus slopes, snowfields, and a small glacier. It is a great loop when combined with the Conrad Kain hut trail but requires glacier travel skills and routefinding experience. It is also possible to scramble Cobalt Lake Spire via the northwest face and north ridge. It is an enjoyable scramble with easy climbing moves on solid rock however you have to cross the glacier to reach the base of the northwest face. It is also possible to continue along ridges to the north to the Rockypoint Basin (see hike #50)

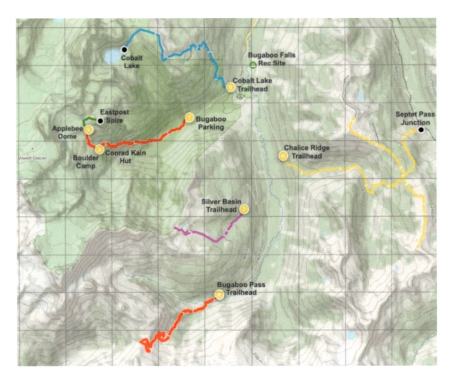

52 Conrad Kain Hut and Applebee Dome

Distance: 10 km
Time: 3-5 hours
Elevation Gain: 991 m

People travel from all over the world to climb the famous granite spires of the Bugaboos. This hike to the Conrad Kain Hut and Applebee Dome takes you to the base of these magnificent and iconic peaks. It can be done as a day hike, however it is such a stellar area that it is worth spending the night. There are several options for overnight accommodation. The Conrad Kain hut can be booked through the Alpine Club of Canada. Camping is available at Boulder Camp near the hut or Applebee Dome, which is higher up on a rocky slab. Campsites are first come, first serve and can be paid onsite. The hut custodian usually collects the camping fees. This hike is in Bugaboo Provincial Park where dogs are not allowed.

Access:
From Radium, drive north to Brisco. Turn left on Brisco Road and cross the multiple channels of the Columbia River. Continue past Patty's Greenhouse and a small gravel pit and turn left at KM 5. Go uphill. At KM 7 turn right

on Bugaboo FSR - the kilometers reset to 0 here. Stay right at Km 11.5, following the signs for CMH. Turn right at KM 36.9 onto a rougher, narrower road. The trailhead is at the end of this this road, about 2.7 km from the junction.

View from Boulder Camp. Photo: AJ McGrath

Trail:

From the parking lot take the well-signed trail which goes up the valley. The first kilometer is fairly flat, going through the forest. Then the real climb starts. The trail winds up steeply, gaining a tree covered moraine, before emerging into an open meadow from which you get your first glimpses of the glaciers and peaks ahead. The trail continues gaining elevation steadily until you reach rocky ledges. A metal ladder has been installed to help gain one of the steeper bluffs. Chains are attached to the rock to help through another exposed steep section. Above this the trail crosses the creek on a metal bridge before climbing through a boulder field. At a junction you can turn left for the Conrad Kain hut and the Boulder campsite, or stay right to continue uphill to Applebee Dome camp. To get to Applebee follow the steep trail through moraines. Below the camp a snow patch may persist well into summer. The campsite is perched high above the valley, in a basin ringed by the iconic Bugaboo Spires, and has fantastic views of the peaks to the south.

Iconic Bugaboo Spire. Photo: AJ McGrath

Options:

At Applebee, you could simply lounge and take in the views. A short walk past the campsite leads to some beautiful tarns. You can also scramble Eastpost Spire (see hike 53).

It is possible to connect to Cobalt Lake via an off trail route. You are required to cross a small glacier and should have crevasse rescue skills and equipment, as well as routefinding skills.

53 Eastpost Spire

Distance: 3 km (from Applebee)
Time: 3-4 hours
Elevation Gain: 530 m

This peak towers above the Applebee campsite, to the northeast. The scrambling route ascends the west ridge. The scrambling is mostly straightforward, and there are cairns to mark the route. The views from the summit are fantastic - you are right across from the famous Snowpatch and Bugaboo Spires. The scrambling is very enjoyable on mostly good rock. A helmet is recommended.

Access:
See Conrad Kain hut/Applebee Dome for road and trail access.

Route:
From Applebee camp take the climbers trail above camp which leads to a small tarn. Go around the tarn to gain the Eastpost - Crescent col. From the col, start up the west ridge. The climbing should be fairly easy, and there are cairns to mark the route. If it feels difficult you are likely off route. The route goes up and right, and then traverses back left on the west ridge, following the easiest way. Near the top you traverse below a rock wall. The last 20 m below the summit is the hardest. You can either stay on the easier but very exposed ridge, or drop down slightly and climb a harder but less exposed gully to the summit. Return the same way.

54 Silver Basin

Distance: 6 km
Time: 2-3 hours
Elevation Gain: 500 m

This a fairly short hike however it is full value - alpine meadows with wildflowers and little tarns, ridges to explore and amazing eye level views of the famous granite spires of the Bugaboos just across the valley. On top of that you get great views of the glaciers of the Quintet Range and Phacelia Pass. This hike is outside Bugaboo Provincial park and therefore dogs are allowed.

Access:
From Radium, drive north to Brisco. Turn left on Brisco Road and cross the multiple channels of the Columbia River. Continue past Patty's Greenhouse and a small gravel pit and turn left at KM 5. Go uphill. At KM 7 turn right on Bugaboo FSR - the kilometers reset to 0 here. Stay right at Km 11.5, following the signs for CMH. Turn left at KM 36.9, the right goes to Bugaboo Provincial Park. Stay right at the next junction and pass by the CMH Bugaboo Lodge and an old airstrip. Continue across a bridge by an outfitter cabin. There is one deep puddle but otherwise the road is in good shape. At KM 39 turn right on Bugaboo South FSR. The road bed is in good shape however there are many deep water bars and high clearance is needed. Drive to the end of this road, enjoying the views of Phacelia pass and the glaciers to the south. Park after 4 km in an open cutblock.

View of the Bugaboos from the ridge above Silver Basin.

Trail:

Follow the decommissioned road to the end of the cutblock where the trail enters the forest. It is well marked and easy to follow as it climbs at a gentle grade through the open forest. After 1.6 km the trail becomes less distinct as it enters the open meadows of Silver Basin. Many options exist here and you may pick up faint bits of trail here and there. To gain the ridge, follow the creek to a slightly steeper slope. At the top of this slope there is a small tarn. From here continue up on rocky ledges to the ridge. Enjoy the fantastic views of the Bugaboo Spires across the valley. You can even see the Conrad Kain hut.

Options:

It is possible to scramble along the ridge to the north to Frenchman Mountain, or south to Anniversary Peak.

55 Chalice Ridge

Distance: 15.6 km
Time: 5-6 hours
Elevation Gain: 1000 m

Chalice Ridge is a splendid area between the Bugaboos and Septet Pass. From the ridge you get excellent views of the Bugaboo Spires. There are many options for exploring this area.

Chalice Ridge

Access

From Radium, drive north to Brisco. Turn left on Brisco Road and cross the multiple channels of the Columbia River. Continue past Patty's Greenhouse and a small gravel pit and turn left at KM 5. Go uphill. At KM 7 turn right on Bugaboo FSR - the kilometers reset to 0 here. Stay right at Km 11.5, following the signs for CMH. Turn left at KM 36.9, the right goes to Bugaboo Provincial Park. Stay left at the next intersection and cross Bugaboo Creek. After crossing the creek go right for Chalice Ridge, the left goes to Septet Pass. At the next junction stay left for Chalice Creek FSR (about 700 m past the Septet-Chalice junction). The road deteriorates and gets more and more overgrown. If necessary park and walk the last kilometer of road.

Chalice Creek Basin

Trail
Begin the Chalice Creek trail by hiking up the old road, which soon turns into a trail, following the creek. After a kilometer the trail crosses the creek. Continue up into the basin. The trail crosses the creek again and shortly afterwards begins climbing up the open forest above towards the ridge. The forest opens into alpine meadows with spectacular views of the granite spires of the Bugaboos. The trail becomes indistinct here. Take note of this spot so you can find the trail again on your way back. There may be bits of flagging. From here, you can either go left towards the ridge to the north, or right for the ridge to the south, or continue straight and descend slightly for another 5 minutes bringing you to a tiny lake.

Option:
It is possible to connect the Chalice Creek Trail with the Septet Pass Trail in the Frances Creek drainage.

56 Bugaboo Pass

Distance: 10 km
Time: 3-4 hours
Elevation Gain: 660 m

Bugaboo Pass is a fantastic hike which sees far fewer people than the nearby Bugaboo Provincial Park. It follows old mining roads to an alpine pass overlooking steep valleys to the west. The glaciers of the Quintet Range are in sight the entire time. In the summer the area is carpeted with wildflowers and in the fall the colors are spectacular. There are several old roads and even some old mining shafts visible at the pass, testament to the mining heritage of the area. In fact, the name Bugaboo was in reference to a dead-end claim, as it turned out that the ore found in the area was of little value.

Bugaboo Pass after a September Snowstorm

Access:
From Radium, drive north to Brisco. Turn left on Brisco Road and cross the multiple channels of the Columbia River. Continue past Patty's Greenhouse and a small gravel pit and turn left at KM 5. Go uphill. At KM 7 turn right on Bugaboo FSR - the kilometers reset to 0 here. Stay right at Km 11.5, following the signs for CMH. Turn left at KM 36.9, the right goes to Bugaboo

Provincial Park. Stay right at the next junction and pass by the CMH Bugaboo Lodge and an old airstrip. Continue across a bridge by an outfitter cabin. There is one deep puddle but otherwise the road is in good shape. Continue all the way to the end, about 8 km from the turnoff to Bugaboo Provincial Park, and park in an old cutblock.

Quintet Range from Bugaboo Pass trail

Trail:
A big log has been laid across the road to mark the end of the road. Start by continuing on the old road to the end of the cutblock where the trail goes into the forest. At first you encounter a couple boggy sections. Soon you come to a bridge over the creek, made up of solid but slippery logs. On the other side of the bridge climb up to an old road bed. After a few hundred meters the trail goes into the forest, leaving the old road bed which is overgrown with alder. The trail climbs through open mature forest before dropping down again to the roadbed, at the edge of an avalanche path. Follow the trail until you reach the creek, with an avalanche path above and a black cliff band high above you. Here the road switchbacks though the trail is not obvious at first. If you miss the switchback and instead climb steeply up next to the creek, don't worry, you'll pick up the trail again higher up. Continue up the switchbacks. As you leave the alder behind the old road gets more and more obvious. Just below the pass there is a junction. You can make a loop by following up one road and coming down the other, and it does not matter which direction you choose. There are several remnants of old roads in the vicinity of the pass. Continue up until you reach the height of land. Enjoy the fantastic views of Rory Creek, the Quintet Range, and Howser Peak.

SPILLIMACHEEN VALLEY

57 Hobo Ridge

Distance: 12.5 km +
Time: 3-4 hours
Elevation Gain: 650 m

The ridge above Hobo Creek is the southernmost extension of the Dogtooth Range. You start high above the Columbia Valley at 1700 m, and without too much effort you gain an expanse of alpine ridges and meadows. The views are fantastic: to the west you look across the Spillimacheen Valley towards Vowell Creek and International Basin, to the east are the prominent Goodsirs and to the south is the expanse of the Columbia Wetlands.

The alpine meadows of Hobo Ridge after a September snowstorm.
Photo: Cam Mclellan

Access:
Drive north from Radium to Parson. Turn left on the Parson River Crossing road. Cross the Columbia River and its back channels and head up the hill on the Spillimacheen FSR. Stay on the main road until KM 7.6. Turn right on the Hobo Creek FSR. Right at the turn you have to drive through a small

ditch. The road is narrow and a bit rutted in spots however 4WD or high clearance is not needed. Stay on the main road, ignoring any side roads, until the end, about 12.5 km from the turnoff. Park in a wide spot before a ditch.

Trail:
The trail is quite obvious, and wide at first. It climbs gradually through open forest. There are a few small creeks and wet spots which are easily avoided. After about 2 kilometres the grade steepens. The trail goes along a ridge overlooking a small tarn on the left before dropping down slightly to cross the outflow from the tarn. After this it climbs more steeply to gain the alpine ridges and meadows above. Continue to the high point from which you can enjoy the panoramic views. There is a radio repeater on the ridge to the right. You can spend some time exploring the ridges and meadows before returning the same way.

Options:
The trail continues along the ridge for a while but eventually peters out. It is possible to connect to the Certainty/Twelve Mile Creek area for a 25+ km off trail ridge walk.

58 Silent Pass

Distance: 4 km
Time: 1-2 hours
Elevation Gain: 360 m

The Silent Pass Trail is a short hike which leads to a pass with fantastic views of the rugged glaciated Selkirk Mountains. It is a fairly easy hike. The trail can also be used to access the Spillimacheen Glacier and can be used to connect to Caribou Creek.

Access:
Drive north from Radium to Parson. Turn left on the Parson River Crossing road. Cross the Columbia River and its back channels and head up the hill on the Spillimacheen FSR. Stay on the main road. At 14 km stay right. At 45.9 km, turn left on the McMurdo Creek FSR and cross the river. Follow the road for another 10.6 km. It is rough and muddy in spots. Park at 55.5 km.

Trail:
Follow the road past the washout for another 800 m until you see the trail to McMurdo branch off to the left in a corner. Continue around the corner to the right. Follow the old road for another 1.9 km. From the end of the road take the obvious trail which starts climbing the hill on the right. The trail climbs steeply at first. Continue through the forest. At one point a snowmobile trail goes through the trees whereas the hiking trail goes left here. Pass a boggy meadow and continue to Silent Lake. Go around the lake and gain the height of land. Across the Duncan Valley you can see the peaks of the Battle Group and Schooner Ridge.

Options:
Continue to wrap around Silent Mountain and go north. It is possible to connect with Caribou Creek from Silent Pass. There is a hiking trail up Caribou Creek but the last 10 km of the road have become so overgrown with alder to be virtually impassable. At this point it is better to access this area from Silent Pass. It is also possible to climb Silent Mountain from Silent Pass, which is a moderate scramble.

Hikes around the Columbia Valley

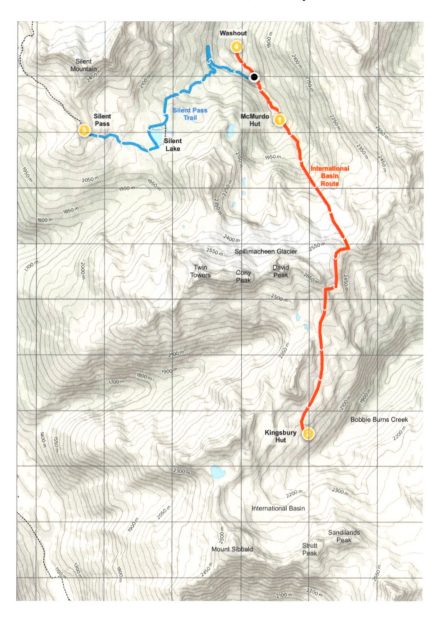

59 International Basin

Distance: 20 km
Time: multi day
Elevation Gain: 1500 m

The route to International Basin requires good route finding skills and should only be attempted by experienced mountaineers. Once in the basin it is worth spending a few days exploring the area. The Columbia Valley Hut Society maintains the Kingsbury Hut which makes an excellent basecamp for exploring the nearby peaks and tarns.

Access:
Drive north from Radium to Parson. Turn right on the Parson River Crossing road. Cross the Columbia River and its back channels on the three bridges and head up the hill on the Spillimacheen FSR. Stay on the main road. At 17 km, take the north fork (ie. stay right.). At 46 km, turn left on the McMurdo Creek FSR and cross the river on a bridge. Follow the road for another 10.4 km. Park at KM 56, where the bridge has been taken out.

Route to International Basin in winter, with the crux marked

Trail:
Follow the road for another kilometer. Where the road curves right, a narrow dirt road goes left, uphill. Follow this road for a kilometer through a marsh to McMurdo Hut. From McMurdo follow a trail into the forest behind the hut. This trail starts gaining elevation and eventually reaches treeline. Cross into a bowl below a pass and continue uphill until you reach the pass. Do not go down the other side of the pass. Rather, continue climbing uphill for another 100 m until you reach a plateau which continues around the side of the mountain. There is a bench below a rocky ridge ahead. Continue on this bench around the corner. You should now see a basin below. Look across the basin to see another plateau on the far side. Climb down into the basin, cross over and find the best spot to climb up steeply, to reach the plateau on the other side. This will be the crux. Make note of this spot for the way back. Continue along the plateau to the southwest. There is a broad peak ahead on the right. Traverse below this peak on the left and continue to lose elevation slightly. Once you reach the end of the peak, you will be above a basin. From here, descend to a gully which leads to the hut, which is located at treeline in a flat meadow.

60 Bald Hills

Distance: 25+ km
Time: 2-3 days
Elevation Gain: 500 m

The Bald Hills are a long drive from Invermere. In fact, you go all the way to the end of the Spillimacheen FSR. It is worth the drive though as it is a fantastic area: alpine meadows with magnificent views of Mount Sir Donald just to the west across the Beaver Valley. In theory it's possible to hike up to Bald Hills and back in a day, however given the long drive and the fairly long hike, it is worthwhile to spend a few days in this beautiful alpine area. If you would like deluxe accommodations, check out Purcell Mountain Lodge, which is located in a splendid location in the Bald Hills with impressive views of the Selkirks to the west. See www.purcellmountainlodge.com/

If camping is more your style there is an excellent spot to camp at Yurt Hollow, though no facilities exist.

View of Mount Sir Donald from Bald Hills

Access:
Drive north from Radium to Parson. Turn right on the Parson River Crossing road. Cross the Columbia River and its back channels on the three bridges and head up the hill on the Spillimacheen FSR. Stay on the main road. At 17 km, take the north fork (ie. stay right.). At 46 km continue straight, the left fork goes to McMurdo. The road deteriorates somewhat after the McMurdo turnoff. Continue to KM 55.8, then take Baird Road FSR on your right. Follow this for another 5 km. You will have amazing views of the peaks around Glacier Circle to the west! If you value the paint on your vehicle you may want to park near KM 59 and walk the last couple kilometers as the alder bushes are quite thick and scrape the sides of your vehicle. There is a sign for

Purcell Lodge parking at KM 60. The trailhead is another kilometer past this sign. It is about 1.5 hours from Parson to the trailhead.

Yurt Hollow with Spillimacheen Glacier in the far distance

Trail:
Initially you follow a wide but rough ATV track. It goes downhill through an old cutblock for a couple hundred meters before entering the forest. After 1.5 km a trail branches off the ATV track to the left. It goes along the creek before coming to an outfitter cabin after another couple hundred meters. If you miss the trail and stay on the ATV track, it will lead to the outfitter cabin as well. The trail continues past the cabin and climbs at a gentle grade through the forest until you reach a creek crossing after another 500 m. The footings for an old bridge are still there but the bridge itself is gone and you must cross on a couple of sketchy planks. On the far side of the bridge take the left hand trail which goes along the Spillimacheen River. The right hand trail just loops back to the horse crossing. Here the trail starts climbing up through fairly open forest. After 6 kilometers you enter an avalanche path and now the country is much more open. You pass close to the river, and also pass by a small tarn. At 7 km there is a junction. Stay right to reach Yurt Hollow. The left hand trail leads to a low pass and gains the Bald Hills. Continue for a couple more kilometers. When you reach the open meadow before Yurt Hollow, stay to the right to avoid a boggy area. At the far end of the meadow the trail crosses a small stream on a big log. There is a wide open area which is a good place to camp. You can even see the Spillimacheen Glacier far to the south. It is 9.5 km to the campsite from the trailhead. To get to the Bald Hills continue by crossing a second stream on a bridge. The remains of the old yurt are visible here. On the other side of this bridge a faint trail leads up to Copperstain Pass, by following the creek, passing the micro hydro station for the lodge. If you take the more obvious trail on the left it leads right past Purcell Lodge to the Bald Hills, about 1.7 km from camp. Please be aware that grizzlies frequent the Bald Hills area and be extra cautious.

Options:

Purcell Mountain Lodge maintains a network of trails throughout this area, however please be courteous towards lodge guests and respect their privacy. From the campsite, hike up Copperstain pass and then gain the Bald Hills plateau, to avoid going right by the lodge. You can hike south along the plateau until you reach the low spot from where you can drop down to the 7k junction and loop back to camp. It is about 10 km. It is also possible to climb Bald Hills Mountain to the north or Copperstain Mountain to the east (see hike #61)

61 Copperstain Mountain

Distance: 8.5 km (from Yurt Hollow)
Time: 3-4 hours
Elevation Gain: 700 m

Copperstain Mountain is a prominent peak just east of the Bald Hills area. It is an easy scramble from Yurt Hollow and has great views.

Access:
See Bald Hills (hike #60)

Starting the hike towards Copperstain Mountain
(visible through the trees on the left)

Trail:
From the camp at Yurt Hollow cross the stream to the east on the big log. Look for a trail about 50 m past the creek crossing. It is faint at first but becomes much more obvious as you go up. It soon enters an avalanche path and then climbs open slopes to gain Grizzly Col. From the col, turn left and climb easily to the summit of Copperstain Mountain. Enjoy the fantastic views of the Dogtooth range to the East and the Selkirks to the west, including the impressive east face of Mount Sir Donald. You can either return the way you came, or for a loop descend the northwest ridge until the trail turns left, off the ridge to drop down to Copperstain Pass. Turn south and follow the creek back to camp.

STANFORD RANGE

62 Diana Lake

Distance: 14 km
Time: 3-4 hours
Elevation Gain: 780 m

Diana Lake is a beautiful blue gem tucked against some impressive rockwalls. The meadows around the lake are filled with larches and wildflowers. Diana Lake Lodge is a family run operation which offers overnight accommodation in a cozy cabin and delicious meals. The lodge also operates a tea house for day hikers. There are not too many places in the mountains where you can stop for a hot lunch and freshly baked goods on a hike! Check the website for opening hours and a menu. https://dianalake.ca/
If you would rather camp, there is a camp site near the lake as well.

Diana Lake from the Judge

Access:
From Radium go 18.5 km north towards Golden. Just after the sign for Luxor Corrals, turn right onto the Kindersley-Pinnacle Forest Service Road. Stay left at 7.3 km on the Pinnacle FSR. Continue on the main road, ignoring any

branches and continue to the trailhead at 24 km, where the road ends. The road bed continues on the other side of the creek, but is deactivated and the bridge has been removed.

Trail:
Follow the trail to the right which leads to an aluminium foot bridge.Turn right onto the old road and follow it for 0.9km. At the bend in the road look for a trail on the right into the woods. Follow this trail for 3km where it turns north and mellows out as it reaches the higher valley elevation. Continue on the trail for 2 km to reach the lake. Follow the trail around the shoreline of Diana Lake up into meadows, or turn right for Diana Lake Lodge.

Options:
A spectacular ridgewalk follows the ridge on the north end of the valley. Follow the trail past the lake and into the meadow to Whitetail Pass. From here the trail turns north (left) and soon the trail disappears as you head up the ridge. At this point you can make your own way, following the ridge. The ridge heads north and then turns to the west, ending in a small peak overlooking the Columbia valley. From here you get great views of the Bugaboos. You can see all the way to Invermere and Lake Windermere and look down onto the wetlands near Spillimacheen. Another option is to scramble the Judge (see hike 63).

63 The Judge (2752 m)

Distance: 6 km (from Diana Lake)
Time: 3 hours
Elevation Gain: 780 m

The Judge is the prominent peak to the east of Diana Lake. It is a great scramble. The last 100 m are on surprisingly good quartzite. From the summit you can see all the way to Lake Windermere.

The ridgewalk approach to the Judge

From Diana Lake, follow the trail through the meadows to Whitetail Pass. From here you turn right and gain elevation to reach a broad ridge which takes you all the way to the base of the peak. The last couple hundred meters involve easy scrambling to gain the summit. The views from the Judge are amazing, as you are able to see Mt. Assiniboine, the Beaverfoot valley, the Kootenay River valley, and the Columbia Valley. Return the way you came.

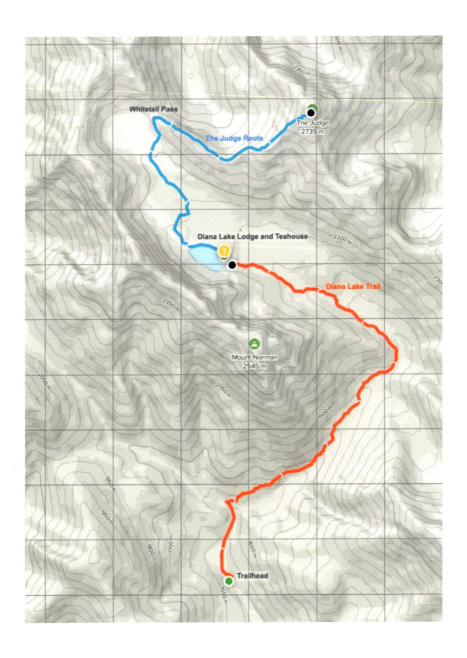

64 Redstreak Creek

Distance: 4.5 km
Time: 1 hour
Elevation Gain: 204 m

The trail along Redstreak Creek is a short hike in the forest. The trail was meant to be connected with the Kimpton Creek trail however that never happened. It is a pleasant outing and good for shoulder season and rainy day hiking. It can also be snowshoed.

Redstreak Creek trail

Access:
From the traffic circle in Radium go east on highway 93 towards Banff. About 3 km past the hot springs look for a small parking area on the right side of the road. It is about 600 m past the Parks Maintenance compound.

Trail:
Cross the creek and continue into the forest. After 2.3 km the trail peters out and becomes more overgrown. Best to turn around at this point.

65 Kimpton Creek

Distance: 10.1 km
Time: 2-3 hours
Elevation Gain: 508 m

The Kimpton creek trail ends somewhat abruptly after 5 km. It is a nice walk nonetheless, going along the creek and eventually crossing several open slopes with decent views. Higher up you can see Kindersley Pass across the valley. It is a good walk for a rainy day.

Upper Kimpton Creek Trail with Kindersley Pass visible in the distance
Photo: Cam Mclellan

Access:
From Radium Hot Springs take Hwy 93 towards Banff. Watch for a small parking spot on the right 8.3 km from Radium. Park here, then walk back along the highway for 100 m to the trailhead.

Trail:
Cross the creek on a good bridge and go into the forest. This is a pleasant shady section. Eventually the trail switchbacks up left and climbs out of the valley. The trail then enters the first of several large open areas. After 5km the trail drops to the creek where it ends. It is a nice spot for a break. Return the same way

66 Kindersley Sinclair Loop

Distance: 16 km
Time: 4-5 hours
Elevation Gain: 1341 m

This is an excellent loop leading over a high alpine pass. Due to frequent bear activity in the area Parks Canada mandates a minimum group size of 4 on this trail. You can hike in either direction however starting up Sinclair Creek and going down Kindersley is nicer as the Kindersley trail is more gentle and easier on the knees going downhill. If you do not have a second vehicle you will have to hike along the highway for 1 km.

Access:
From Radium Hot Springs drive east on Highway 93. Pass the hot springs and continue for another 7.6 km. Look for a small pullout on the right. Leave a vehicle here. Continue to the Sinclair Creek trailhead which is in a sharp curve on the left side 1 km further uphill. Park here.

Trail:
The trail follows the left side of the creek for a while before crossing over a log bridge and then steadily gains elevation, eventually breaking out into flower filled alpine meadows. The trail then contours below the hillside to

gain Kindersley Pass. From the pass enjoy the spectacular views to the west and south. The trail continues north around the flank of Mount Kindersley. Do not be tempted to drop straight down from the pass as the slopes are quite steep. The trail goes to the right, gradually dropping to the pass below. This area is a wildlife corridor so make lots of noise. From the pass the trail turns south and eventually goes into the forest. It is a pleasant, gentle grade. Lower down the trail breaks out into a wide avalanche path filled with wildflowers before going back into the forest and finally emerging onto the highway.

Nearing the top of Kindersley Pass

67 Cobb Lake

Distance: 5 km
Time: 2-3 hours
Elevation Gain: 246 m

Cobb Lake is a short hike through the woods to a small lake. It is a good hike for kids, and can be snowshoed as well.

Access:

From Radium drive east on Highway 93 towards Banff. Look for a pullout on the right, 16 km east of Radium. If you get to the viewpoint you have gone too far.

Trail:

From the trailhead the trail goes downhill to Swede Creek, crosses and starts going up the other side. You go through a nice mature forest before reaching this pleasant little lake. Return the way you came.

68 Dog Lake

Distance: 5.1 km
Time: 2-3 km
Elevation Gain: 333m

Dog Lake is a short hike to a scenic lake in the Kootenay valley. It's a great hike for kids. It is also a good hike if you want to stretch your legs on a drive through the park. The trail is well built and well graded. Kids love the suspension bridge across the Kootenay River.

Access:
From Radium Hot Springs drive east on Highway 93 for 27 km to the well signed Dog Lake trailhead.

Trail:
The trail starts out quite flat, winding through the forest. Within 100 m you pass through the McLeod Meadows campground. Shortly afterwards you will reach the suspension bridge, followed by a second bridge over the Kootenay River. The trail then climbs gently up a forested ridge before dropping down slightly to the lake. Enjoy the views of Mitchell Ridge (hike # 80).

Dog Lake with Mitchell Ridge in the background (hike #80)

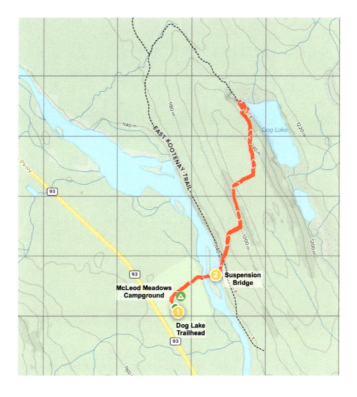

69 Redstreak Mountain (scramble)

Distance: 16 km
Time: 5-7 hours
Elevation Gain: 1610 m

This peak is visible from many places in the valley. It is easily recognized by its prominent band of red limestone. A steep but well flagged trail leads most of the way to the summit via the west ridge. The crux is a short section of limestone slab which requires a few climbing moves. A shorter version skips the scrambling and leads to a prominent viewpoint on the ridge. On a clear day you can see the entirety of the Columbia Valley spread out in front of you, from Mount Baker near Cranbrook all the way to Golden. Across the valley you are almost eye level with Mount Nelson, Mount Farnham and Farnham Tower. In the distance you can see the glaciers of Earl Grey Pass. It is a fantastic spot!

View of the Columbia Valley from the summit of Redstreak Mountain

Access:
It is no longer possible to start this hike at Radium Springs Resort as the landowners do not permit access. Instead, you have to start at Redstreak Campground in Radium. Drive up the hill behind the Radium Visitor's Centre to Redstreak Campground. Pass the entrance booth and take the first right to a picnic area. Park here.

Trail:
Take the Restoration Trail which begins right at the picnic area. After about 75 m it crosses a gravel road. Turn left onto this road which continues through an open area for about 1.5 km. Continue past a metal gate and look for a trail on your left after 30 m. It goes up the hillside and leads to a cutline which is the boundary between Kootenay National Park and the Golf

Course. It runs parallel to the mountain. Follow this cutline for about 50 m, then take a flagged trail on your left which goes into tight dense trees. It climbs up slightly to a bench and then contours for about 750 m. Eventually it intersects another cutline, which goes towards the mountain. You will see KNP boundary markers. Follow the trail up the cutline, rapidly gaining elevation. At about 1280 m elevation the trail goes left, climbing up the hillside. Follow a flagged trail all the way to the west ridge. From here you could go left to the first viewpoint on the ridge however it is worthwhile to go right and push a little higher. Follow the open ridge, climbing steeply until you reach a prominent high point. If you are not interested in scrambling you could turn around here, after enjoying the fantastic views.

To continue to the summit, the trail descends from this highpoint and goes into the forest. It starts climbing up again after a low point on the ridge and then stays on the ridge except for a couple spots where it goes left to go around rock bluffs. Once you reach the very red rock band the trail descends left for about 100 m until it starts climbing up again. When it rejoins the ridge, it goes left to avoid a small cliff and then climbs up to the base of the crux. A 2 bolt anchor and a fixed rope have made this crux a lot less committing, however be sure to check out the integrity of the rope before trusting it. Above the crux continue to climb until you reach the sub peak. To get to the true summit, continue over the sub peak, go down and then right, around another rock buttress, and then climb up a short scree gully. At the top of the scree gully continue right and up until you reach the summit. To descend, reverse the route. Be sure to reward yourself with an ice cream cone from Leo Burrito's - you've earned it!

70 Mount Swansea

Distance: 12 km (shorter options exist)
Time: 3-4 hours
Elevation Gain: 750 m

The Swansea South Ridge hiking trail overlooking Invermere
Photo: Corinna Strauss

Mount Swansea is a small peak just east of Windermere. The slopes of the mountain are covered in a network of trails, which are often the earliest to be snow free in the spring. The lower elevations of the trail network may be hiked year round. In the winter, the slope below the upper summit can have significant snow on it, and often has a large cornice. If you are traveling here in the winter, be aware that there may be an avalanche risk.

Views from both the lower and the main summit are excellent. The summit is also used as a launch by paragliders. A rough road goes most of the way to the top however it is gated from September to early summer. Mount Swansea is somewhat notorious for ticks in the spring so be sure to do a thorough tick check after hiking here. There are designated hiking and biking trails. Do not hike on designated downhill mountain bike trails as bikers travel at high speed. A collision between a hiker and a biker could end badly for both.

The name Swansea refers to the peak's mining history. There was a copper mine on Mount Swansea until the 1950s, and the ore was taken by boat down the Columbia River to Golden and then by rail to Vancouver. From there it was sent to Wales via the Panama Canal, to the Swansea smelter (see "Mines in the Windermere Valley" by the Windermere Valley Archives and Museum for more).

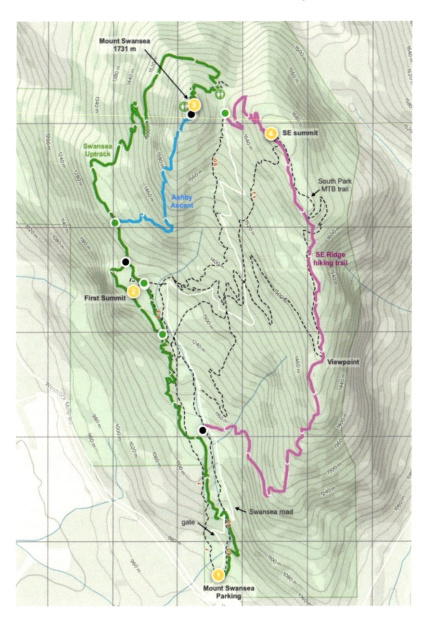

Access:

From Invermere drive south on highway 93 for 3 km. Turn left on Windermere Loop road and continue for 3.3 km. Turn left towards Mount Swansea and cross the Westroc Mine road into the Swansea Parking lot. On weekends the parking lot can fill up quickly. Do not park on the mine road. If the parking lot is full, park on Windermere Loop road and be sure not to block the road or any driveways.

157

Trail:

From the parking lot you have a few options for your hike.

For a shorter hike hike the Swansea Tower loop to the first viewpoint. From the parking lot it is 2.8 kms one way to the tower lookout with 285 meters elevation. If you wish to continue to the summit of Mount Swansea from here follow a trail past the picnic tables that goes down to the right. This trail brings you to the backside of the tower lookout. Continue to the Swansea Trail (Upper). From the tower lookout to the summit the trail is 3.8 km and 375 m elevation gain. Watch for mountain bike trails crossing the hiking trail. The trails are well signed. As you ascend you will share part of the uptrack for mountain bikers. As you are hiking on Swansea uptrack you will reach another signed junction for hikers only that is labeled Ashby's Ascent. This steep trail will take you directly to the summit, bypassing the road. From the sign Ashby's Ascent it is 1.4 km and 400 m elevation gain. Once you reach the summit of Mt. Swansea, catch your breath and take in the views. You have a few options to get back down the mountain. The obvious options are going back down the same way you hiked up. Or from the summit descend the back side of the summit from the Swansea (Upper) Trail and once you reach the upper parking lot follow the road for a few hundred meters. Then, you will see a sign for the SE Ridge trail. Ascend this trail to the SE ridge lookout and descend the SE ridge to the parking lot. Take a close look at the map at the trail kiosk or use an app on your phone as there are several other trails to reach the parking lot. The trail is 3.6 kms and 600 meters descent. The SE Ridge trail may also be used to hike up and for me (CS) personally,

this is my favorite way to go because there are not too many other trails to confuse you! You may also descend via the Swansea mountain road. If you choose this, watch for traffic. When the gate is closed the road is a peaceful option.

View from Mount Swansea summit. Photo: Corinna Strauss

71 Four Points Mountain

Distance: 6.7 km
Time: 3 hours
Elevation Gain: 937 m

This hike is a great short and steep outing that is close to Invermere and can easily be fit into a half day. It is at a lower elevation and is a good shoulder season outing.

Access:
From Invermere drive south on highway 93 for 3 km. Turn left on Windermere Loop road and continue for 3.3 km. Turn left towards Mount Swansea and then immediately turn right onto the Westroc Mine road, before the Swansea parking lot. This road is unpaved but well maintained. Park right before the kilometer 7 sign at a small pullout on the right side of the road. Make sure you are tucked off the road as much as possible. Watch for mine trucks and remember they have the right away. The big trucks move fast!

Trail:
From your car, follow a faint path that leads towards the creek and look for a log crossing with a wire cable above the log. If you cannot find it, keep looking! Cross it, and after this, the trail is more defined. This trail is steep and gains approximately 900m elevation in 3.5 kms. This is a local trail and it is unmaintained. Be prepared to route find as the trail diminishes in places.

72 Mount Pinto

Distance: 8.7 km
Time: 3-4 hours
Elevation Gain: 960 m

Summit of Mount Pinto

Mount Pinto is well visible from Invermere. It is a relatively short but steep hike with easy scrambling near the top. It has great views of the Columbia Valley to the west and Mount Assiniboine to the east.

Access:

From Invermere drive south on highway 93 for 3 km. Turn left on Windermere Loop road and continue for 3.3 km. Turn left towards Mount Swansea and then immediately turn right onto the Westroc Mine road, before the Swansea parking lot. This road is unpaved but well maintained. Expect mining trucks to be moving fast and give them the right of way. After 3 km go left up the Bernais Road towards Mount Pinto. The road switchbacks through an old mine site. After 7 km on this road go right and after another kilometer go left. The parking lot is in a landing after another 400 m at the end of this road.

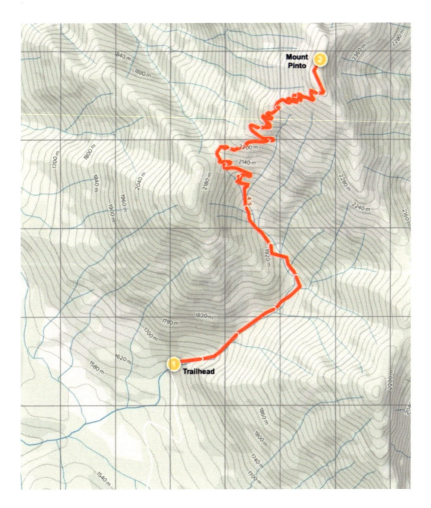

Trail:

This trail was recently improved by the Summit Trail Makers Society, with the help of Columbia Basin Trust funding. From your car gain the well defined trail on the east side of the parking area. For 2 km the trail moves through forest and leads to the base of the avalanche paths below Pinto Mountain. The trail continues up to the end of the meadow / avalanche path where it enters the forest with a large orange hiker sign attached to a tree. Continue past the avalanche paths to the north forested ridge. The trail following the ridge towards the peak becomes indistinct. A short, steep, exposed scramble to the peak affords expansive views. Proceed to the ridge and exposed areas with caution.

73 Mount Bryan

Distance: 6.5 km
Time: 4 hours
Elevation Gain: 950 m

Mount Bryan is another local gem of a hike. It is a prominent peak roughly between Mount Tegart and Mount Pinto. It is steep and requires good route finding skills. All wheel drive is necessary to access the trailhead.

Access:
From highway 93/95 head east on Windermere Loop road as you would for Swansea Mountain but continue onto Westroc Mine road. About 2 km past the Twin Lakes/Windermere Wells rec site look for an unsigned logging road at coordinates N50.48519, W115.86735. Turn left. Follow this road up. Ignore a road to the right and continue upwards. Park in a
n opening at the end (N50.48476, W115.85225).

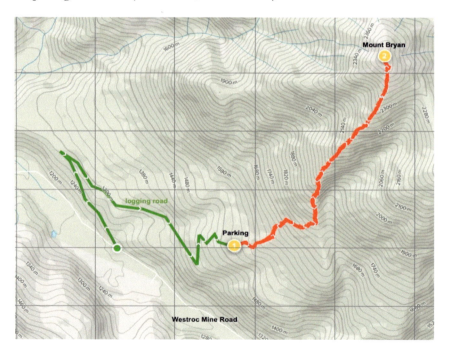

Route:
There is no distinct trail. Navigate upwards through a cutblock, then bushwack through juniper bushes to gain the south ridge of Mt. Bryan. The beginning of a faint trail up the ridge towards the summit is at N50.48758,

W115.84291. From here you will see a rocky and craggy view and continue up the steep and faint trail towards the summit. Before you summit you will reach an opening full of Whitebark pine trees and from here continue up the sub alpine terrain to the summit to find a cairn. Descend as you came up. A special thanks to Herb Weller for maintaining this "trail".

Reaching the summit of Mount Bryan in late October.
Photo: Corinna Strauss

74 Pedley Pass

Distance: Complete loop: 10.2 km
Time: Complete loop: 5-6 hours
Elevation Gain: Complete loop 450 m

Pedley Pass is an incredibly popular hike, for very good reason. It is fairly close to Invermere, and the parking lot is at high elevation. With moderate effort you get to a beautiful alpine area carpeted with wildflowers in the summer. There are several options for hiking Pedley Pass. A 10 km loop trail goes along the ridge. To the pass and back is 4 km, while the trail from the pass to the tarn is 2 km return. The longest option takes the trail to the pass, continues to the tarn, and returns via the loop trail. If you are doing the loop it is recommended to go counterclockwise. The climb up through Bumpy Meadows is more gentle and shady than the switchbacks from the parking lot. The switchback trail faces south, and can be a hot climb in the summer. From the ridge you get fantastic views of Mount Assiniboine to the north.

Approaching the tarn at Pedley Pass

Access:
From Invermere drive south on highway 93 for 3 km. Turn left on Windermere Loop road and continue for 3.3 km. Turn left towards Mount

Swansea and then immediately turn right onto the Westroc Mine road. Do not enter the Swansea parking lot. This road is unpaved but well maintained. Expect mining trucks to be moving fast and give them the right of way. At KM 13 continue straight past the mine. The road is much narrower and rougher now. Stay on the main road, ignoring any spurs. Continue all the way to the end. The last kilometer is quite rough and bumpy, however the road does not require high clearance.

Trail:
From the parking lot take the trail to the right which follows a gentle grade for several hundred meters before starting the climb. After a kilometer the trail crosses an open area called Bumpy Meadows. At the far end of the meadow the trail again climbs up towards the pass. The forest starts thinning out as you near the pass. At the pass you can take the trail to the right to get to the tarn. The trail meanders through the forest for a few hundred meters before contouring slightly down into the small basin. The tarn is in this basin. To scramble Mount Aeneas continue past the tarn (see hike #75).

From the pass you can also hike in the opposite direction, taking the trail to the left. After 500 meters you reach "the overlook", a high point on the ridge. This is also a great destination. To continue the loop, continue along the ridge, dropping down slightly and then climbing up again to the next high point. This is a fantastic ridgewalk with great views in every direction. At the far end of the ridge the trail drops down and enters the forest. It crosses an open slope and then starts the switchbacks (18!) back to the parking lot.

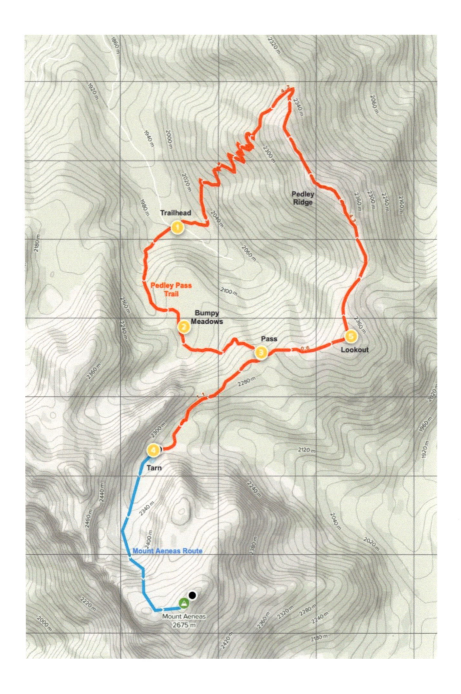

75 Mount Aeneas

Distance: 8.6 km
Time: 4-5 hours
Elevation Gain: 834 m

Mount Aeneas is named for a character in Greek mythology. To avoid any awkward mispronunciations make sure you emphasize the second syllable! It is a fairly straightforward scramble from Pedley Pass and the summit has a fantastic view of the entire Columbia Valley. Keep an eye out for goats.

Access:
See Pedley Pass (hike #74)

Mount Aeneas scrambling route. Photo: Cam Mclellan

Route:
From the top of Pedley Pass follow the trail to the tarn. Go around the tarn on a faint trail which peters out in the talus. Continue towards the back of the valley and turn left towards Mount Aeneas. You will find several gullies below the summit plateau. The right most gully is likely the easiest. An ice axe and crampons may be useful early in the season if there is still snow in the gully. A helmet is also a good idea. Climb up the gully to gain a broad plateau below the summit. Cross the plateau to gain the west ridge. Climb up the west ridge to the summit. Return the same way.

Option:
It is possible to traverse from Mount Aeneas to Chisel Peak via connecting ridges.

76 Chisel Peak

Distance: 10 km
Time: 6-8 hours
Elevation Gain: 1300 m

Chisel Peak (which is marked as Indian Head Mountain on older maps) is a prominent peak on the eastern skyline of Invermere. It is an excellent and challenging scramble.

Chisel Peak - the scrambling route follows the right hand skyline

Access:
From Invermere drive south on highway 93 for 13km. Turn left on Kootenay Road #3 and immediately turn right. Continue for 2 km, then turn left onto Madias FSR. This road is very rough and you need 4WD, high clearance and good backroad driving skills. The first part of the road climbs up through open forest. Maneuver around deep ruts. At 1 km stay right. At 2 km, turn left and continue uphill. The road contours around into the valley. There are several narrow spots and washouts. Park at a deep washout 10 km from the highway.

Route:

Continue up the old road past the washout. After 1.5 km cross another washout. Look for a trail on the other side of this washout. It begins to climb steeply through the forest. The trail eventually goes into an open area and may be hard to follow in spots but once you are in the open continue climbing up towards a pass, directly west of Chisel Peak. Once you gain the pass continue left towards the west ridge of Chisel Peal. You may pick up faint trails as you continue climbing steadily towards the summit. The route stays on or close to the west ridge the entire way up. From the first summit you can traverse along a narrow ridge to the second summit. The rock is generally fairly good limestone. Return the way you came up.

77 Mount Tegart (2381m)

Distance: 7.2 km
Time: 2-3 hours
Elevation Gain: 930 m

Mount Tegart is easily visible from the Columbia Valley. It is a short but worthwhile scramble. From the summit you get fantastic views of the nearby Chisel Peak, and Columbia Lake, Lake Windermere, and the Purcells to the west.

Access:
From Invermere drive south on highway 93 for 13km. Turn left on Kootenay Road #3 and immediately turn right. Continue for 2 km, then turn left onto Madias FSR. This road is very rough and you need 4WD, high clearance and good back road driving skills. The first part of the road climbs up through open forest. Maneuver around deep ruts. At 1 km stay right. At 2 km, turn left and continue uphill. The road contours around into the valley. There are several narrow spots and washouts. About 6 km from the highway you come to an ATV track which goes up a draw. Park here

Trail:
Hike up the ATV track which eventually turns into a trail. Climb fairly steadily until you reach the bottom of several avalanche paths below the summit of Mount Tegart. Continue up the valley to the farthest avalanche path and follow faint trails up as you climb up the avalanche path towards the summit. The trails eventually peter out. Continue climbing on grassy slopes until you gain the ridge. Follow it to the right to the summit. The last part of the summit requires a few scrambling moves. It is easier on the left, up a gully.

Summit Ridge of Mount Tegart. Photo: Cam Mclellan

78 Fairmont Mountain (scramble)

Distance: 3 km
Time: 2 hours
Elevation Gain: 500 m

This peak is at the southern end of the Fairmont Range. From Fairmont it looks like it would be a difficult climb. However, a road goes most of the way up the backside making it a fairly straightforward scramble via the south ridge.

Fairmont Mountain from Columbia Lake. The scramble follows the right hand skyline.

Access:
From Canal Flats take the Kootenay Forest Service Road, which starts behind the post office at the end of Burns Ave. Go for about 16 km and look for Dry Creek FSR on your left. This road is quite long, and rough in places, requiring 4WD. Continue on Dry Creek FSR for about 15 km, staying on the main road the whole way. It climbs to 2000m. Near the end of the road it passes below a small forested pass, directly south of Fairmont Mountain. Park below the pass.

Route:

From the road follow a small gully towards the pass. At the height of land, turn right and start traversing on the forested ridge towards Fairmont Mountain. The forest is fairly open. Once you reach the talus slopes the going is pretty straightforward. Continue up towards a talus filled gully which goes all the way to the summit. Watch for loose rock. Descend the same way.

CROSS RIVER – PALLISER RIVER

79 Nipika - Natural Bridge

Distance: 11 km (many other options)
Time: 3 hours
Elevation Gain: 332 m

Nipika is an eco resort which has an extensive trail network open to the public. In the winter the trails are groomed for cross country skiing, snowshoeing and fatbiking. In the summer the trails are great for hiking, trail running and mountain biking. Please note that trail fees apply in the winter and donations are accepted in the summer to offset trail maintenance costs.

Check out www.nipika.com for more information. The resort is dog friendly. There are many possible options - a hike to the natural bridge and back is a fine choice. Stop at the day lodge to pick up a map.

Access:
From Radium drive north on highway 93 towards Banff. As you descend into the Kootenay Valley, look for Settlers Road on the right, about 20 km from Radium. Follow Settlers Road for 12 km, staying left on the Cross-Palliser FSR. After another kilometer, cross the bridge and Nipika is a few hundred meters on the left.

Trail:
From the parking lot, go past the big open meadow. Take Rufus Ramble, go past the warming cabin and then to Teen Spirit. Then take Jesus Murphy to Blow your Chamois, which goes along the river. It turns into Spin Doctor. Go left on Shirtless Tuesday. When you reach a road, turn left and in a short distance you come to the natural bridge. A man made bridge goes over the natural bridge, looking down into the impressive canyon of the Cross River. From the bridge, take North Riverside Loop to North Fatbike trail, then turn left on Roxy Roller. Go left on Rattle your stuff back to Rufus Ramble. This loop is about 10.4 km.

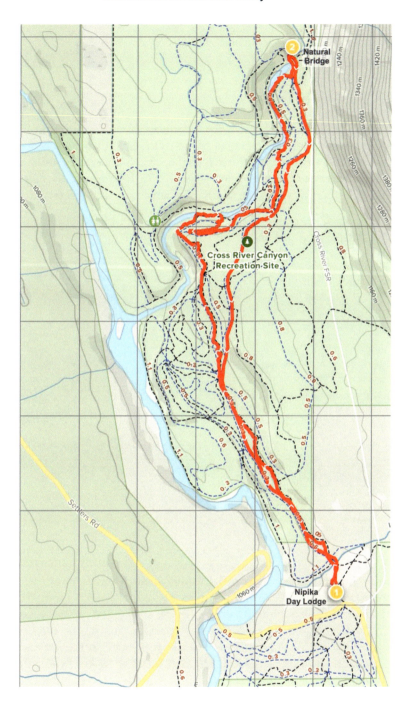

80 Mitchell Ridge

Distance: 10.5 km
Time: 4-5 hours
Elevation Gain: 995 m

Mitchell Ridge is visible from the Kootenay valley viewpoint on Hwy 93. It is a fantastic ridgewalk with great views of the Kootenay River valley, Mount Assiniboine, and even the Purcells to the west. It is a bit of a grunt, especially the first 2 km, and there are no switchbacks. It is best to do this one on a cooler day, as you climb the south ridge which has little shade and no water.

Mitchell Ridge

Access:
From Radium drive north on highway 93 towards Banff. As you descend into the Kootenay Valley, look for Settlers Road on the right, about 20 km from Radium. Follow Settlers Road for 12 km, staying left on the Cross-Palliser FSR. After another kilometer, cross the bridge. Stay left on the Cross River FSR at 14 km. At 20.5 km take Corral Creek road on the left and set your odometer. Stay right at 1.4 km. Stay right again at 1.7 km (where the sign on the left says Corral Creek South). At 2.1 km stay left on Corral Creek West. At 5 km turn left onto a grassy road. Continue for another 1.8 km until the road ends in an old landing. The last 1.8 km has several waterbars which might challenge cars with less clearance.

Trail:
The trail starts at the end of the landing. Initially it climbs up an old skid road before going along the Kootenay National Park boundary line and continues climbing up the ridge. The first 2 km climb fairly relentlessly before the terrain eases off. The first summit is at 4.2 km. The second summit is at 5.4 km.

Options:
It is possible to continue along the ridge for as long as your time and energy allow.

81 Assiniboine Lake

Distance: 14 km
Time: 4-5 hours
Elevation Gain: 665 m

Assiniboine Lake is to the south of the iconic peak. It is often used by mountaineers to access the mountain, via a small glacier. The lake itself is a tranquil, beautiful spot and has nice camp sites.

Access:

From Radium drive north on highway 93 towards Banff. As you descend into the Kootenay Valley, look for Settlers Road on the right, about 20 km from Radium. Follow Settlers Road for 12 km, staying left on the Cross-Palliser FSR. After another kilometer, cross the bridge. At Km 14 stay left on the Cross River FSR. You are now on a mine haul road used by the Baymag mine at the head of the valley. Expect mining trucks on this road and give them a wide berth. At KM 37.5, just before the Baymag mine, turn right, onto a narrower road. The trailhead is after a second creek crossing on the left in a corner.

Assiniboine Lake

Trail:

The trail initially follows an old skid road through second growth forest before climbing up a dry slope. It then follows the creek fairly closely. At 3.5 km take a cable and log bridge across a side creek. After another kilometer, a faint trail to the right goes to Lunette Lake. It is worth the short detour as you get a good look at the southwest face of Mount Assiniboine. Once back on the main trail it is only another 1.3 km to Assiniboine Lake. There is a nice campsite by the lake.

Options:

Experienced mountaineers can continue further up the valley. You can climb over a small but crevassed glacier to access the Hind Hut below the north ridge of Mount Assiniboine. From there, you can drop down via the "Gmoser Highway" to Lake Magog and Assiniboine Lodge.

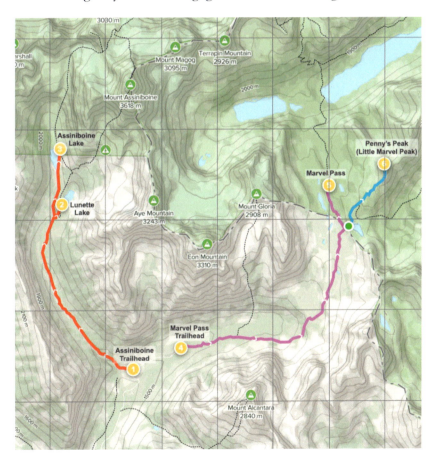

82 Marvel Pass

Distance: 14 km
Time: 4-5 hours
Elevation Gain: 760 m

Marvel Pass is a beautiful subalpine area with meadows and flowers. A small lake right at the pass, Aurora Lake is a worthwhile destination. Marvel Pass can also be used to access the Mount Assiniboine area via Wonder Pass. This area is a wildlife corridor and is frequented by bears. Stay alert and carry bear spray.

Access:
From Radium drive north on highway 93 towards Banff. As you descend into the Kootenay Valley, look for Settlers Road on the right, about 20 km from Radium. Follow Settlers Road for 12 km, staying left on the Cross-Palliser FSR. After another kilometer, cross the bridge. At Km 14 stay left on the Cross River FSR. You are now on a mine haul road used by the Baymag mine at the head of the valley. Expect mining trucks on this road and give them a wide berth. At KM 37.5, just before the Baymag mine, turn right, onto a narrower road. The trailhead is at the end of the road, about 1.5 km past the Assiniboine Lake trailhead.

Trail:
The trail starts on the right side of the road and drops down to the creek. After crossing the creek continue up the valley through fairly open forest. After an hour you reach a junction. Stay right and continue towards the back of the valley. Eventually, you will reach a boulder field from where you get great views of Mt Eon, towering above you to the northwest. Begin contouring around the valley towards the pass. As you near the pass, the terrain opens up more. In spots the trail may be less distinct but there should be cairns to mark the way. At the pass, you will encounter the Banff National Park boundary marker. Shortly after the boundary you will reach Aurora Lake.

Options:
You can continue across the pass and downhill to Marvel Lake, which is 4 km away. From Marvel Lake it is another 4 km to Wonder Pass via a fairly strenuous climb. From Wonder Pass it is 2 km to Assiniboine Lake. Otherwise, you can climb Little Marvel Peak (Penny's Peak) from the pass (see hike #83). It is also possible to continue around the east side of Marvel Peak to Owl Lake in Banff National Park

Marvel Pass

83 Marvel Peak/Penny's Peak 2559m

Distance: 17.2 km
Time: 5-7 hours
Elevation Gain: 1007 m

While Marvel Pass is a great destination on its own, it is highly recommended to combine it with an ascent of Penny's Peak (Little Marvel Peak). The views of Mount Assiniboine, Lake Gloria, Marvel Lake and Mount Eon are well worth the extra effort. Penny's Peak is a fairly straightforward scramble, requiring only some route finding sense. To get to the summit of Marvel peak itself is slightly more involved, though no more than 3rd class climbing.

Marvel Pass and Mount Assiniboine from Penny's Peak.
Photo: Matt Hobbs (Penny's dad)

Access:
Start at Marvel Pass

Route:
From Aurora Lake go through open forest towards the south ridge of Marvel peak. Small cliff bands can be easily avoided by going around. As you gain elevation the views of the area improve. The terrain also opens up. The route is not well defined but just continue uphill and eventually you reach the south ridge. Continue climbing on decent scree to the summit.

Option:
From Penny's Peak it is possible to continue to the true summit of Marvel Peak. Drop down from Penny's peak via scree slopes for about 200 m to gain the Penny's/Marvel Col. Continue towards the left hand side of the cliff while side hilling. This section is loose. Try to maintain elevation. Once you reach the cliff continue up a loose scree ramp to the summit ridge, from where moderate scrambling leads to the summit.

84 Whiteman Pass

Distance: 10 km
Time: 3-4 hours
Elevation Gain: 689 m

This is a fairly short hike which leads to the continental divide and just over the boundary into Banff National Park. The hike itself is enjoyable, as it leads to flowery subalpine meadows and a little tarn. It also gives easy access to a

remote area with plenty of potential for scrambling and exploration.

Access:
From Radium drive north on highway 93 towards Banff. As you descend into the Kootenay Valley, look for Settlers Road on the right, about 20 km from Radium. Follow Settlers Road for 12 km, staying left on the Cross-Palliser FSR. After another kilometer, cross the bridge. Stay left on the Cross River road at 14 km. Continue on this road until kilometer 32.5. Cross a bridge and then take

the next right, a narrower, rougher road. This road will lead to the upper Cross River. The old road at km 32 is washed out. Continue on the Cross River road until Km 46 and park at a hairpin corner. Talus Lodge is just south of here and you may see cars parked on the road.

Trail:

From the hairpin corner a well flagged trail leads straight ahead. It drops slightly and leads to the creek. Follow the right side of the creek, gaining elevation steadily. About halfway to the pass, cross the creek on a good bridge and continue climbing. After another kilometer the terrain levels out and you cross a small creek. From here the trail climbs to the height of land, the Continental Divide and the Banff Park boundary. The trail drops down again and emerges into open meadows with two small tarns. Return the way you came or spend several hours exploring the sparkling blue lake just south of the pass or the tucked away lake just north of the pass. There is also potential to scramble several peaks in the vicinity.

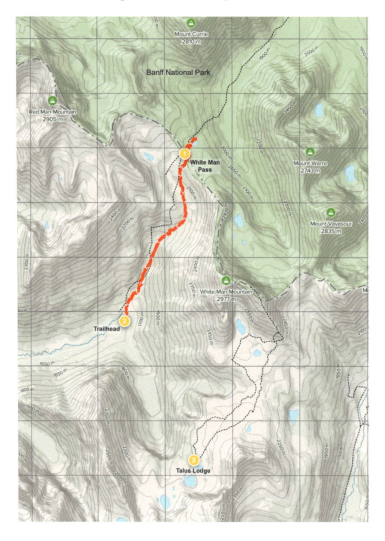

85 Ralph Lake

Distance: 9 km
Time: 3-4 hours
Elevation Gain: 902 m

Ralph Lake is a beautiful alpine lake at the northern end of Height of the Rockies Provincial Park, tucked under the mighty peaks of the Royal Group. The lake is surrounded by lovely meadows and has very good fishing. There are several options for easy scrambles in the area. The hike to Ralph Lake is short, but quite steep. It can easily be done in a day but it is also worthwhile to camp at the lake (no facilities) and spend a day or two exploring the area. It is also possible to traverse from Ralph Lake to Queen Mary Lake via a challenging but rewarding off trail route.

Access:
From Radium drive east on highway 93 towards Banff. As you descend into the Kootenay valley, look for Settlers Road on the right, about 20 km from Radium. Follow Settlers Road for 12 km, staying left on the Cross-Palliser FSR. After another kilometer, cross the bridge. Stay right on the Palliser FSR at KM 14. Stay left at KM 36. At KM 40 turn left on the Albert FSR. At KM 51 you pass through a beautiful cedar grove, which is quite rare in the Rockies. Continue to KM 58 and turn right on Shag Main (ignore Lower Shag at KM 57). Continue for one more km to the trailhead. The last kilometer is quite steep and rough and requires 4WD. You can park before the hill and walk up the last section of road.

Trail:

The trail switchbacks up through a new cutblock before going into the forest. Once you enter the forest the trail climbs very steeply up the hillside, through lush cedar and hemlock. After a kilometer the grade eases off and the trail contours high above the valley bottom before rounding the corner to the Ralph Lake drainage. As you near the headwall, the grade steepens again as the terrain starts opening up. Eventually you pass below a limestone wall with a small cave and some hanging ferns. Immediately after, the trail climbs up through a short rock step before levelling out for the last few hundred meters to the lake. The best spot to cross the outflow creek is right at the lake. A faint trail goes around the left lake shore, while a more obvious trail goes around the right. There is a beautiful campsite right at the outflow. If you go counterclockwise around the lake you will see an old A frame cabin a short distance above the shore. It could make an emergency shelter in a pinch but is in fairly rough shape. There are decent camp spots near the cabin as well.

Options:

The peak to the north of the lake (Queen Mary NW3) makes for an interesting scramble. To access it, walk around the north shore of the lake, into the meadows until you are almost right below a pass which connects this peak to Mount Queen Mary. Walk past a tiny tarn and start going uphill more steeply until you gain the pass. Turn left and wander along the ridgeline towards the summit, enjoying views of Mount Assiniboine to the north. The summit itself is quite interesting. Look over the edge to see a castle of broken rock below. To descend, return the way you came or descend steeply on grassy slopes directly to the lake below.

Another great scramble is the peak to the south of Ralph Lake (Queen Mary W2). It is accessed via the pass southwest of the lake, which is also the route to Queen Mary Lake. Either continue on the lakeshore trail all the way to the meadows and follow the creek, which comes from the pass, uphill, or go ⅔ of the way around the lake and follow another creek uphill which leads to a small tarn. Follow the open boulder fields below the peak to another tarn from which the pass is easily gained. From the pass, turn right (west) and walk uphill. The summit looks quite steep but as you get closer the angle is a lot less frightening and there is an easy route to the summit. The views from this peak are truly astounding. You can see Mount Assiniboine to the north, the high peaks of the Royal Group immediately to the east, Mount Harrison to the south and even the familiar silhouettes of Mount Nelson and Farnham tower to the west.

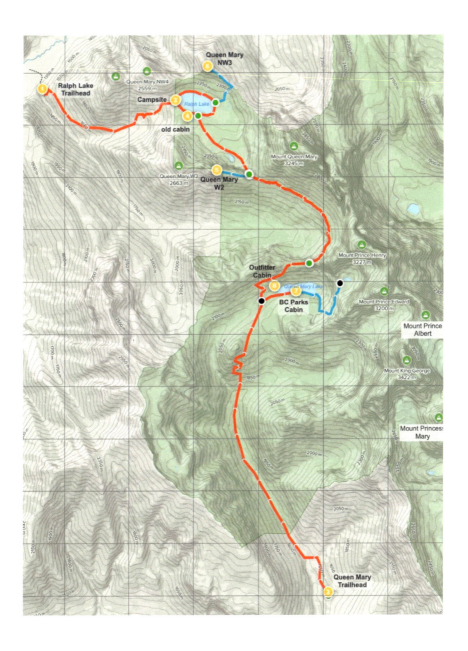

86 Queen Mary Lake

Distance: 20.5 km
Time: multi day
Elevation Gain: 995 m

Queen Mary Lake is a turquoise gem, tucked under the high peaks of the Royal Group, in Height of the Rockies Provincial Park. It has good fishing. There is both a private guide outfitter cabin and a BC Parks Cabin (first come, first serve) at the lake as well as informal campsites.

There are two ways to get to Queen Mary Lake. You can either start in the Palliser valley, and follow a horse trail to the lake, or traverse over from Ralph Lake via a challenging but rewarding off trail route. In the past the horse trail has had a bad reputation due to multiple river crossings. However, if you go later in the summer when water levels are lower the route is actually quite reasonable. If you have two vehicles, doing a north to south traverse from Ralph Lake to Queen Mary Lake and out via the horse trail is an excellent option.

Queen Mary Lake. Photo: Cam Mclellan.

Access:
To get to the Queen Mary Lake trailhead drive east from Radium on highway 93 towards Banff. As you descend into the Kootenay valley, look for Settlers

Road on the right, about 20 km from Radium. Follow Settlers Road for 12 km, staying left on the Cross-Palliser FSR. After another kilometer, cross the bridge. Stay right on the Palliser FSR at KM 14. Stay left at KM 36. At KM 54 turn left and follow this road to the trailhead. It is well signed. Park by the trail sign, just before a washout.
For access to Ralph Lake see hike #85.

Trail:
The trail goes downhill for a few hundred meters. After 1.6km you reach Queen Mary creek and follow it upstream. The trail crosses the creek multiple times. After about 6 km it starts climbing the hillside steeply before dropping slightly again to reach the lake. Continue along the right side of the lake to reach the BC Parks cabin. There are good campsites nearby.

To access Queen Mary Lake from Ralph Lake requires good off trail hiking and route finding skills. The route looks improbable but is actually quite reasonable, though it involves a good amount of sidehilling. From Ralph Lake gain the pass to the southwest, either by continuing on the lakeshore trail all the way to the meadows and following the creek which comes from the pass uphill, or else by going two thirds of the way around the lake and following another creek uphill through the forest. It leads to a small tarn. Follow the open boulder fields to another tarn from which the pass is easily gained. From this pass you can see another pass to the southeast. Queen Mary Lake is on the other side of this pass. The route is marked on the photo below. Resist the temptation to drop down from the pass. The route crosses several gullies which are much steeper walled lower down and are easier to cross higher up. The route generally contours at 2400 m elevation and passes above the grassy green cliffs at the head of the basin. It continues on a ledge above black cliffs and continues contouring around a scree basin to a diagonal ledge which gains the pass through a cliff band. There are occasional goat trails to follow. At the pass continue south along a faint trail to the far end of the pass until you see a trail dropping down the south side. This trail contours around some limestone buttresses. Just past this you can see an opening going directly to the lake below. This is an option to get to Queen Mary Lake quickly, but steeply. Otherwise, the trail gradually continues to lose elevation and reaches the valley bottom some distance from the lake. When you reach the valley, it connects with the Queen Mary trail. Turn Left and follow it to the lake. It takes about 4 hours from Ralph Lake to Queen Mary Lake via this route.

The traverse route between Ralph Lake and Queen Mary Lake

Option:

From Queen Mary Lake it is possible to scramble up to the top of the waterfall at the far end of the lake, to a magnificent limestone amphitheatre with fantastic views of Queen Mary Lake. Continue on the lakeshore trail to the far end of the lake. Hike uphill for 50 m to a hidden little tarn. Continue up and right, following the little stream which feeds into the tarn. Continue uphill on a talus cone to the cliffs above, heading for a snowpatch below the cliffs. You should see a yellow rock band above. Go almost all the way to the cliffs until you can traverse fairly easily to the left. You will reach a fairly broad ledge with goat trails. It drops down slightly and then climbs up again to reach the amphitheatre at the top of the waterfall. Follow a series of small waterfalls and pools to a small tarn. It is about an hour from Queen Mary Lake.

87 Limestone Lakes

Distance: 35.2 km
Time: multi day
Elevation Gain: 2018 m

The magnificent Limestone Lakes are accessed via a unique Karst plateau. This interesting geological feature was created by the interaction between water and limestone, resulting in cracks, crevices, spiky tufts and little canyons. The rock is very sharp and can easily cut up a dog's paws. It is a good idea to bring booties if you are bringing a dog on this hike. There is a good trail to Sylvan Pass, from where you are required to travel off trail to Limestone Lakes.

Access:
To get to the Limestone Lakes/Joffre Creek trailhead drive east from Radium on highway 93 towards Banff. As you descend into the Kootenay valley, look for Settlers Road on the right, about 20 km from Radium.

Follow Settlers Road for 12 km, staying left on the Cross-Palliser FSR. After another kilometer, cross the bridge. Stay right on the Palliser FSR at KM 14. Stay left at KM 36 and continue all the way to the end of this road, to KM 61.

Trail: The trail goes into an old cutblock and after a short while reaches the Joffre Creek crossing. You may have to ford, or if you are lucky you may be able to cross on some logs slightly upstream. Do not ford the river if water levels are high. Once on the other side the trail continues through the forest for another kilometer. Go right at a junction and the trail starts climbing up the hillside, eventually going along Joffre Creek through a canyon. The trail stays in the forest for the next several kilometers. You pass by a small campsite though there is much better camping further along. Eventually the terrain opens up and you see Sylvan Pass up ahead, with Mount Joffre towering above. From the pass, climb the ridge to your right, to a peak called the Nub. Enjoy the views of the White River drainage to the south. Continue down the far side (south) to a small pass below. This is where the off trail route starts.

Continue to climb down to the west, avoiding small cliff bands until you reach the Karst plateau below. Once on the flats start heading in a generally

southerly direction, towards a broad plateau to the south. Gain elevation through small cliff bands, and follow in the same direction as the cliffs. Once you reach the height of land continue down the other side until you see the lakes ahead. Walk downhill on grassy slopes until you reach the lake.

There are many excellent spots to camp but no facilities. Please preserve this unique environment and leave no trace. Fires are not allowed in the Limestone Lakes area.

Options:

While it is possible to hike to Limestone Lakes and back in two long days, it is well worth spending a day or two exploring the area. You can wander higher up the basin to the upper lakes and to another pass or scramble on the hillsides around the

basin, looking out for goats. You can also traverse to Russell Lake (see hike #94).

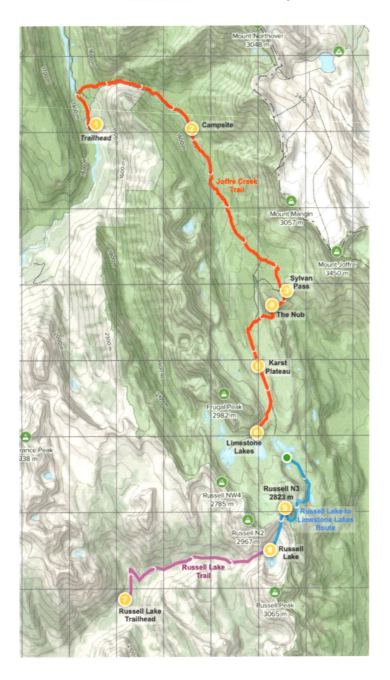

WHITESWAN AND BEYOND

88 Gibraltar Lookout

Distance: 8.5 km
Time: 3-4 hours
Elevation Gain: 785 m

This is a steep trail to an inactive BC Fire lookout station with superb views of the Kootenay and White River Valleys.

Access:
Driving time is approximately one hour from Canal Flats. Travel with an adequate AWD vehicle and be aware of logging trucks. From Canal Flats, drive south and turn onto the Whiteswan lake FSR. Set your odometer to zero here. At 11km turn left onto Kootenay Bypass road. At 17 kms, turn right onto Kootenay - Eastside FSR. There are many spur roads, stay on the main road. At 23 km take a left fork (the right fork is marked Kootenay Glen FSR). At 25 km, take a left at the Y junction (right is marked Nine Mile Main FSR). At 33 km, the next Y junction, turn left. (right is marked Kootenay Mia North FSR - deactivated). At 34 km, bypass an unmarked junction to the left, follow Kootenay Main to the right. Immediately look for a faint road through the grass to the left (within 20 m). There is a green hiker sign on a tree to the left. The sign is marking the start of the Kootenay-Gibraltar FSR. Follow this road for 7kms and park at approximately 41 kms. The Kootenay - Gibraltar FSR is narrow and steep, it may seem unlikely at times. There is a turn around at 2.5 km up but nowhere to turn around beyond that if another vehicle is met.

Photo: Corinna Strauss

194

Trail:
From your vehicle follow the trail and shortly after you start take the fork to the right. Hike up a steep trail in a lodgepole pine forest for about 1.5 kms. After you leave the forest the trail traverses a steep hillside and to a small col, this is approximately 2.5 kms. From here, do not go straight up, but traverse the open slope below the fire lookout. Continue this trail until it meets the ridge that will provide access to the fire lookout. Enjoy the views!

Options:
From Gibraltar Lookout it is possible to continue along the ridgeline south. It is even possible to connect all the way to Ptarmigan Lake (see hike #91), via ridges. This requires experience and route finding skills.

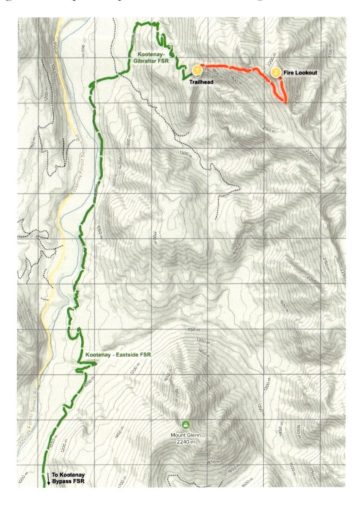

89 Whiteswan Ridge

Distance: 8.5 km
Time: 4-5 hours
Elevation Gain: 910 m

This is a fantastic ridgewalk close to Whiteswan Lake. You get great views of Mount Harrison, the southernmost 11,000er in the Rockies. On a clear day you can see far up the White and Kootenay River valleys and you can even see the Purcells. The

turquoise and dark blue waters of Whiteswan Lake are always in sight, far below. There is no water on this trail. Go on a cooler day or bring lots of water. This ridge is grizzly habitat and you will likely see bear digs. Bring bear spray and stay alert.

Access:
From Canal Flats drive 5 km south and turn off at the Whiteswan FSR. Drive past Lussier Hot Springs and Whiteswan Lake and turn right just past KM 29 onto White-Blackfoot FSR, and set your odometer to 0. Take Inlet Creek FSR which goes straight at 1.5km, where Blackfoot curves left. At 4.2 km take the next obvious left. This road has serious waterbars which might challenge a car with low clearance. Stay on the main road. It switchbacks first right, then left. At the next switchback to the right, go straight. This is at 9.1 km from the turnoff. The trailhead is at the end of this spur, after 500m.

Trail:
The trail begins at the far end of the landing. It climbs up through replanted forest for 200 m before entering mature forest. The trail is quite steep for the first 1.5 km. After the first steep bit you finally break out of the forest onto an open ridge. You will see the "Great Wall" up ahead - an impressive limestone feature. Climb towards the base of this wall. The trail follows right along the base of the rock wall, so close that you can put your hands on the rock. At the far end of the rock wall climb up a short steep pitch to the broad ridge above. It is very worthwhile to turn left and scramble easily up to the

top of the Great Wall. You get fantastic views of Whiteswan Lake and the White River valley. Retrace your steps to where you came up the ridge and continue along the ridge to the south. The going is easiest if you follow the ridge crest closely. In a few spots you may have to drop to the left to avoid small bluffs. After another kilometer along the ridge you gain another high point with a cairn on it. Soak up the views of the peaks and valleys in all directions.

The Great Wall. Photo: Cam Mclellan

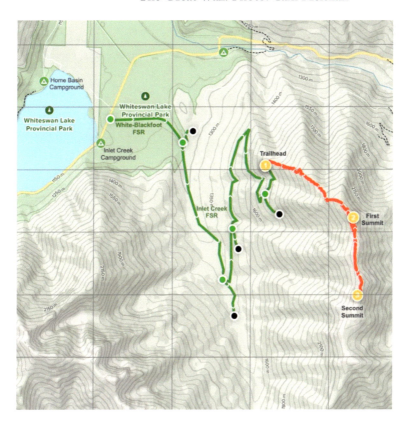

90 Whiteswan Northshore Trail

Distance: 10-20 km
Time: 3-6 hours
Elevation Gain: 200 m

The north shore trail goes all the way from Alces/Moose Lake Campground to Home Basin Campground. It is a pleasant hike which travels through Douglas Fir forest along the shoreline. You get great views of the clear blue waters of Whiteswan Lake and the surrounding mountains. It is a good shoulder season or rainy day hike as it is at low elevation. Unless you have two vehicles, you will have to go out and back. There is a campsite at Cave Creek, about 3 km from Home Basin or 5 km from Alces Lake.

Alces (Moose) Lake

Access:
From Canal Flats drive 5 km south and turn off at the Whiteswan FSR. Drive on this road for 21 km, passing Lussier Hot Springs at KM 17.5. Turn into the Alces Lake campground and park at the day use parking lot.
Alternatively, drive all the way to the far end of the lake and turn left towards Home Basin campground just past the 30 km marker. Drive down this road for 1 km. After the bridge over the creek turn left and continue to Home Basin campground.

Trail:

The trail starts at the far end of the Alces Lake campground. At first it winds around Alces Lake. It comes fairly close to the road again at the far end of the lake, and you could access the trail here as well though the first part along Alces Lake is very enjoyable. The trail follows the north shore with some ups and downs. Shortly after crossing Cave Creek, there is a detour along the creek to Cave Creek Campground. It is a nice spot for a break. Continue all the way to Home Basin if you wish or turn around here. Some people continue all the way around the lake. However, you have to walk on a busy and dusty logging road for 10 km. This option is not recommended.

91 Ptarmigan Lake

Distance: 12 km
Time: 3-4 hours
Elevation Gain: 700 m

This is a pleasant hike to a deep blue lake. From the lake it is possible to scramble White Knight Peak or explore the basins and ridgelines to the north. The lake also has good fishing.

Access:

From Canal Flats drive 5 km south and turn off at the Whiteswan FSR. Drive on this road for 30 km, passing Lussier Hot Springs and Whiteswan Lake. At the far end of the lake turn left towards Home Basin campground just past the 30 km marker. Drive down this road for 1 km. After the bridge over the creek turn right onto Moscow FSR. Continue on this road until KM 36 then turn left onto Ptarmigan Main - there is a sign that says road closed however you can continue up this road for about 500 m before parking at the first curve. The trail is just ahead.

Trail:

It is possible to bike the first 3 km. The trail follows an old roadbed and climbs pleasantly along the creek in an open valley. Eventually you come to an overgrown landing. Cross the creek and continue along the old road until you reach the edge of a mature forest. Continue through the lush forest, past a couple small waterfalls. You climb a short section before the trail levels again. The last kilometer to the lake the trail climbs quite steeply between limestone slabs. There are a few campsites at the lake.

201

92 White Knight Peak

Distance: 5 km (from Ptarmigan Lake)
Time: 3-4 hours
Elevation Gain: 700 m

White Knight Peak forms the backdrop to Ptarmigan Lake. It is a moderate scramble. The crux involves accessing the summit ridge (see arrow). It may in the summer when the crux gully still has some snow in it and an ice axe may be useful in that case.

Access:
Via Ptarmigan Lake

Route:
Cross the outlet of Ptarmigan Lake on some logs. There is a faint trail which gains a ridge before petering out. The lake shore may be easier traveling but is steep in spots and might require getting your feet wet. Regardless, work your way around the lake to the inlet. Follow the inlet creek uphill until you come to a big open meadow below a scree slope. which leads into a basin. Climb up this scree slope, then look for one of several exit gullies above to the low point on the ridge (see arrow). This is the crux. It either necessitates climbing up on snow, or negotiating a moat. Later in the season it may be loose rock. Once you have gained the east ridge follow it to the summit of White Knight Peak. It is also possible to continue to the summit of Blue Knight Peak just to the north.

Return the way you came.

93 Graves Lookout

Distance: 11.6 km
Time: 4-5 hours
Elevation Gain: 883 m

The 2017 White River fire destroyed the fire lookout however this is still a great hike. As you hike through the recently burnt forest you see that many wildflowers have sprung up after the fire. The views are much more open as a result of the burn, though on a hot day there is little shade. From the top you have great views of the Bull River, North White and Height of the Rockies.

Access:
Drive 5 km south of Canal Flats and turn left on the Whiteswan FSR. Continue on this road until km 32.5 then turn right onto the White River FSR. At 43.5 stay right on the main road. At 45 km stay left on the White Middle Fork. At km 48.7 look for a washed out road which goes uphill on the right along a cutblock. Park on the main road here and start hiking up the old road.

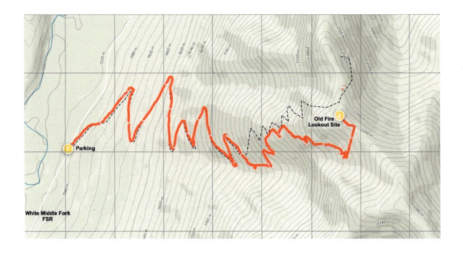

Trail:
Follow the old roadbed for 2 km, then the trail begins climbing up the steep mountain side. Once you gain the ridge turn left to go to the old lookout site. Return the way you came. It is also possible to hike further up the ridge above the old lookout.

Former Graves Fire lookout

94 Russell Lake

Distance: 15 km
Time: 1-2 days
Elevation Gain: 505 m
Map Page 193

Russell Lake is a deep blue lake nestled in a valley ringed by peaks. It is a beautiful, remote area which does not see much traffic. It is worth spending a few days exploring the area. There is good camping at Russell Lake. As the crow flies, Russell Lake is quite close to Limestone Lakes. However, the trailheads for these two areas are far from each other. The Russell Lake trailhead is at the end of the north fork of the White River, past Whiteswan Lake, whereas the Limestone Lakes trailhead is at the end of the Palliser FSR. It is possible to connect the two areas via an off trail route. It is also possible to scramble the peak above the lake, Russell N3. From its summit you get a great view of the Limestone Lakes.

Russell Lake. Photo: Austin Stone

Access:
Drive 5 km south of Canal Flats and turn left on the Whiteswan FSR. Continue on this road until km 32.5 then turn right onto the White River FSR. At 43.5 go left, towards the Graves Creek Rec Site. Continue on the White North Fork FSR, driving through an area burned in the 2017 White River Fire, which covered 25,000 hectares. Continue up this valley on a fairly good road, until KM 72. Look for a rougher road going right. There may be a couple washed out sections on this road. Continue all the way to the end

where the road ends at a creek crossing, about 6.5 km from the turnoff. The last section will likely require 4WD and higher clearance.

Trail:
Cross the creek and go left on the other side, taking an old road. Follow this road for about 3 km, past several old cut blocks. From the end of the road, continue on a trail which goes into the forest. After 1 km cross a boggy area below an avalanche path. The trail becomes indistinct here but you should be able to find it again on the far side. Pass through a second slide path. Continue along the left side of the creek passing a small tarn. Eventually you leave the forest behind, to reach Russell Lake.

Options:
From Russell Lake it is possible to scramble up Russell Peak N3. Continue past the lake, up the meadows to the north. The meadows will give way to scree slopes and the angle starts steepening. From the summit you get great views of the Limestone Lakes. You can continue to Limestone Lakes by descending to the east to a tarn. From the tarn, go north along the edge of a small glacier then go east around some cliff bands to descend to a slightly bigger lake. From here, travel via a broad bench to Limestone Lakes to the north.

View of Russell Lake from Russell Peak. Photo: Austin Stone

Top of the World Provincial Park (Hikes 95 – 100)

This popular provincial park is at the end of a long logging road, however it is well worth the drive. The trail to Fish Lake (#95) is an easy hike and is great for families and novice backpackers. There are several excellent day hikes which can be done from Fish Lake (#96 - 100), as well as several good scrambles. The extensive karst plateau and meadows east of Fish Lake make for interesting off trail rambling. It is possible to hike or bike to Fish Lake for the day, however it is also worth spending a few days exploring the area. Mountain biking is allowed on the Fish Lake trail. Not surprisingly, the lake has good fishing.

There is a BC Parks cabin at Fish Lake which is first come, first serve ($15/person or $30/family per night). In addition, there is a campsite on the lake, with tent pads, benches and food caches ($5/person/night). The fees can be paid ahead of time through the BC Parks website however campsites cannot be reserved. There is a campsite at Coyote Creek as well.

Access:
Go 5 km south of Canal Flats and turn left towards Whiteswan Provincial Park. At kilometer 21.3 go right, up a hill towards Top of the World Provincial Park. At kilometer 29.6, turn right and cross Coyote Creek. Continue straight at kilometer 30.7, staying on the main road to the trailhead at kilometer 52.

Fish Lake
Trail.
Photo:
Cam
Mclellan

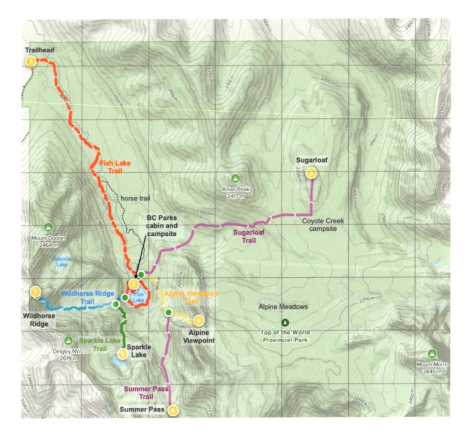

95 Fish Lake - Top of the World Provincial Park

Distance: 12. 6 km
Time: 4-5 hours
Elevation Gain: 495 m

Trail:
The trail starts by going downhill slightly before turning right to go along the Lussier River. The trail is well graded and fairly wide. It stays in the forest for the first four kilometers before coming to an open meadow.
After the meadow you start climbing up towards Fish Lake though the trail is never steep.

Options:
For a short outing, take the lakeshore trail around the lake. It is 2 km and takes 30 minutes. For longer options see the next several hikes.

96 Sparkle Lake - Top of the World Provincial Park

Distance: round trip 5.6 km (from Fish Lake)
Time: 1-2 hours
Elevation Gain: 360 m

Sparkle Lake is a popular short day hike from Fish Lake. It is a beautiful little lake, sitting in an alpine basin about 400 m above Fish Lake. Please note that camping is not allowed at Sparkle Lake.

Trail:
From the cabin go counter clockwise around the lake. Cross the Lussier River. After 600 m from the cabin you come to a junction. Go right, and begin climbing uphill through the forest. You gain elevation quickly via several switchbacks. At the top of the climb there is another junction. Go left here and cross the open slide path. Reenter the forest briefly, then skirt the edge of a talus field. Climb across open slopes to the basin which contains the lake. The trail becomes indistinct here. Try to stay on the rocks to avoid erosion in the meadows.

Option:
From the lake is it possible to scramble onto the ridges above.

97 Wildhorse Ridge - Top of the World Provincial Park

Distance: 6.4 km
Time: 2-3 hours
Elevation Gain: 640 m

The Wildhorse Ridge trail climbs up the valley just to the west of Fish Lake. From the ridge you get great views of Mount Doolan and Dolomite Lake. You are on an open, south facing slope so be sure to bring lots of water.

Trail:
From the cabin go counter clockwise around the lake. Cross the Lussier River. After 600 m from the cabin you come to a junction. Go right, and begin climbing uphill through the forest. You gain elevation quickly via several switchbacks. At the top of the climb there is another junction. Continue straight here, the trail on the left goes to Sparkle Lake. Continue along the edge of a boulder field and switchback up to the ridge.

98 Alpine Viewpoint - Top of the World Provincial Park

Distance: 6.4 km
Time: 2-3 hours
Elevation Gain: 600 m

This hike climbs up the scree slope and ridge across the lake. It is a bit of a grunt but is worth it. You get amazing views of Fish Lake, the Lussier valley and Mount Morro across an expansive alpine plateau.

Trail:
From the cabin backtrack towards the trailhead for about 200m. At the first junction, go right. At the next junction continue straight rather than taking the lakeshore trail. Shortly afterwards there is another junction. Go right for the Alpine Viewpoint. After a few hundred meters you reach the slide path. After this, there is no well defined trail. Climb up the scree slope to the ridge. Be mindful of rockfall, especially if there are parties ahead of you or behind you.

The Alpine Viewpoint trail climbs up the scree slope opposite the lake.
Photo: Cam Mclellan

Option:
It is possible to make a loop by climbing up to the Alpine Viewpoint, descending to the plateau on the other side and traveling off trail across the meadows to Coyote Creek camp and returning to Fish Lake via the Coyote Creek trail (8-10km loop). It is also possible to continue across the plateau to Mount Morro, which can be climbed via the South Ridge (3rd class).

99 Summer Pass - Top of the World Provincial Park

Distance: 8 km
Time: 3-4 hours
Elevation Gain: 430 m

Summer Pass is a long pass south of Fish Lake. The pass is filled with flowers and is a wildlife corridor. Carry bear spray and stay alert. There is a small tarn below the west face of Deception Peak.

Trail:
From the cabin backtrack towards the trailhead for 200 m. At the first junction, go right. At the next junction continue straight rather than taking the lakeshore trail. Shortly afterwards there is another junction. Go right for the Alpine Viewpoint trail. After a few hundred meters you reach the slide path. Cross the slide path and continue contouring around the flanks of Mount Deception. The route is initially in the forest but soon the trees thin out and the views improve. From the pass you can look south towards the impressive Empire State and Chrysler Peaks

Options:
From the pass it is possible to loop around the south flanks of Deception Peak to gain the alpine meadows area. You can make a loop by returning via the Alpine Viewpoint Route, with some routefinding involved. It is also possible to climb the east ridge of Mount Dingley (3rd class) from Summer Pass.

100 Sugarloaf - Top of the World Provincial Park

Distance: 14 km
Time: 5-6 hours
Elevation Gain: 368 m

The Sugarloaf is a nondescript looking rounded peak near the Coyote Creek campsite. However, from the summit you get panoramic views of the upper Lussier River valley. Be sure to carry plenty of water for this hike.

Trail:
From the cabin backtrack 200 m to a junction. Go right. At the next junction go straight rather than taking the lakeshore trail. Shortly afterwards the trail splits. Go left here. Continue on the Coyote Creek trail until 5.6 km where the Sugarloaf Trail branches off left and continues to the top of the Sugarloaf.

101 Connor Lakes

Distance: 14.4 km
Time: 5-6 hours
Elevation Gain: 480 m

The Connor Lakes are a string of lakes located at the southern end of Height of the Rockies Provincial Park. These beautiful lakes are remote and surprisingly large, and the drive to the trailhead alone feels like an adventure. The largest of the three lakes is 3 km long and there is good fishing. A small BC Parks cabin at the north end of the largest lake is available first come, first serve. It has a wood stove, outhouse and some basic kitchen supplies though no cooking stove or mattresses. There are two ways to approach Connor Lakes. The Mayuk Creek trail is described here. The Forsyth Creek trail is near Elkford, which is outside of the area covered by this book. It is possible to hike to Connor Lakes and back in a day, however given the long drive and the beautiful location it is well worth staying a night or two.

Connor Lakes.
Photo: Cam
Mclellan

Access:
The road to the Mayuk Creek trailhead is in fairly good shape, other than the usual washboard and potholes, and a car should be able to make it for all but the last 1.5 km. Drive 5 km south of Canal Flats and turn left on the Whiteswan FSR. Continue on this road until km 32.5 then turn right onto the White River FSR. At 43.5 stay right on the main road. At 45 km stay left on the White Middle Fork. Continue on this road all the way to the end. You will be driving through the area burned in the 2017 White River Fire, which covered 25,000 hectares. At 59 km you pass by the Mt Forsythe rec site and at 68 km pass the Mayuk Creek rec site. Look up the White River valley for views of Mount Joffre. Just after the rec site stay right. At 70.5 km the road is washed out. A 4WD vehicle will be able to get past the washout but cars should park here. The trailhead is at 72 km. It is a long drive, about 2 hours from the highway.

Trail:

The trail starts by going through an area burnt in 2003. Trees have grown back but they are still fairly small. The grade is mostly gentle with a few steeper sections. Look for goats on the ledges above you. At 2 km from the trailhead you pass by an open area where the creek meanders lazily through a marsh. At 4 km the trail crosses a washout. After several ups and downs you reach the pass at 6.1 km. If you look back down the valley you will see the impressive looking Catalan Peak in the distance and a pretty little tarn below you which is not otherwise visible from the trail. From the pass you also get your first glimpses of the Connor Lakes. Continue downhill to the

lake. At the bottom of the hill stay right for the hiker's trail, and shortly after go left to reach the cabin. The Forsyth Creek trail joins from the right. Cross the bridge and go along the shore to reach the cabin. There are good spots to camp in front of the cabin.

Options:

A trail behind the cabin to the left goes to the upper Connor Lake, from

where you get spectacular views of the glaciated Mount Abruzzi up the valley.

Experienced mountaineers can climb Mount Abruzzi via its south glacier, which is gentle and straightforward however does require glacier travel skills. The trail peters out after the upper Connor Lake and routefinding skills are required. The smallest lake, which is between the other two lakes, can be reached via some faint trails along the creek. The Forsyth Creek trail can be used to get to the far side of the largest Connor Lake.

PREMIER LAKE

102 Shark Tooth

Distance: 12 km
Time: 4-5 hours
Elevation Gain: 900 m

This enjoyable hike climbs into an alpine bowl filled with wildflowers and eventually gains a ridge from where the impressive limestone formation called the Shark Tooth can be seen. The ridges lend themselves to scrambling and exploring. The trailhead is also near the Ram Creek warm springs which are located 1.4 km from the road, accessible by a decommissioned road.

Access:

From Canal Flats drive south on Hwy 93/95 and turn left on Premier Lake road. Stay left on Sheep Creek road and right at the next junction, Sheep creek north (left goes to Island Pond Road). Cross the creek (in late summer and fall salmon can be seen spawning just upstream from the bridge). Shortly after the bridge the road turns to gravel and is called the Ram Creek FSR. Continue up this road. Stay right at 5 km. At 9 km the road curves left. Straight ahead is the decommissioned road which leads to the warm springs. Continue left and go up the hill. About 2 km after the warm springs trail you have to cross a fairly committing creek. Adventurous drivers can continue up the road for another 1.5 km, staying right at a junction. Or else park just before the creek and walk up the last 1.5 km. There is also a very faint trail which goes up left just past the creek and cuts out some road walking.

Trail:

Once you reach the end of the road, the trail goes straight ahead and shortly after crosses the creek. It goes along beside the creek and gains elevation at a moderate grade. Eventually the trail comes out into the open basin. It becomes much less distinct. There are also many game trails in this basin. You want to gain the pass ahead on the left. Following the dry creek bed is

easier walking than contouring the grassy slopes on game trails. Once you reach the pass you will see the obvious Shark Tooth. You can traverse left on the ridge to a viewpoint or go right to the base of the Shark Tooth. There are many possibilities for rambling and exploring. Return the way you came.

103 Saddleback Ridge

Distance: 15.2 km
Time: 7-8 hours
Elevation Gain: 1540 m

This challenging trail leads to the ridge east of Premier Lake. The trail is not as frequently maintained as the trails in the provincial park and there may be some blow down. However, the views from the ridge are amazing and it is a worthwhile hike for those looking for a good challenge.

Access:
From Canal Flats drive south on highway 93 for 26 km. Turn left onto Sheep Creek Road. After 650 m turn left towards Premier Lake Road. After 7 km turn right onto Wasa Sheep Creek road. Continue on this road, which turns to gravel, all the way to the end, about 7 km. It is well signed for Premier Lake. Park at the first parking area that you see across from the playground.

Views of Premier Lake from Saddleback Ridge. Photo: Corinna Strauss

Trail:

You can access the trail either between campsites 25 and 27, or walk into the first loop on your right and access the trail between sites 46 and 47. These two trails meet after 200 m. Continue straight, passing the short Cat's Eyes Lakes trail on the right. Right before you reach Yankee Lake at approximately 2 km take a right and get on Saddleback Trail. Stay on this trail and follow it for approximately another 8 km to the col south of Travois Peak. This is a beautiful, steep and long hike.

Travois Col. Photo: Corinna Strauss

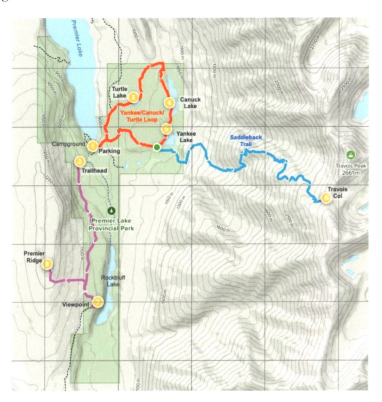

104 Yankee Canuck Turtle Lakes

Distance: 6.2 km
Time: 2 hours
Elevation Gain: 250 m

This is a short hike in Premier Lake Provincial Park which goes past three small lakes through an open forest. It is a great early season hike and good for kids. Bikes are also allowed on this trail.

Access:
From Canal Flats drive south on highway 93 for 26 km. Turn left onto Sheep Creek Road. After 650 m turn left towards Premier Lake Road. After 7 km turn right onto Wasa Sheep Creek road. Continue on this road, which turns to gravel, all the way to the end, about 7 km. It is signed for Premier Lake. As you enter the campground, there is a parking spot with an information sign on your right. If this is full, you may have to park at the day use area by the beach and walk back on the road.

Trail:
You can access the trails either between campsites 25 and 27, or walk into the first loop on your right and access the trail between sites 46 and 47. These two trails meet after 200 m. Continue straight, passing the short Cat's Eyes Lakes trail on the right. At the next junction you can go either left or right - depending on whether you want to hike clockwise or counterclockwise. If you go right (counterclockwise) you will go through a recently cleared area. Yankee Lake will be the first lake you pass, then Canuck Lake and finally Turtle Lake before looping back to the junction. If you are lucky you may see western painted turtles at Turtle Lake.

105 Premier Ridge

Distance: 8 km
Time: 2-3 hours
Elevation Gain: 300 m

The sparsely treed ridge to the west of Premier Lake is a pleasant place to hike in the springtime when the first crocuses and shooting stars are just poking out. There is a dirt road which leads from Premier Lake to the Rockbluff Lake overlook but once you get onto the ridge there are no real trails and you must find your own way. The first part can also be biked.

Access:
From Canal Flats drive south on highway 93 for 26 km. Turn left onto Sheep Creek Road. After 650 m turn left towards Premier Lake Road. After 7 km turn right onto Wasa Sheep Creek road. Continue on this road, which turns to gravel, all the way to the end, about 7 km. The trailhead is about 200 m before you enter the campground, on the right.

Trail:
Follow the dirt road on the right towards Premier Ridge. After 3 km on this road you get to the Rockbluff Lake viewpoint. From here, you can go right, up the hill towards the top of the ridge. There is no trail but the forest is open and easy traveling. Once you reach the ridge go right and follow it to the top. From the top, go downhill to the east to get back to the road you started on.

RESOURCES

First Aid Courses
- Wilderness Medical Associates, https://wmacanada.com/
- Rocky Mountain Adventure Medicine, https://adventuremed.ca
- Slipstream, https://wildernessfirstaid.ca

Equipment
- Revolutions Gear, Outdoor Gear Consignment Store, 1225 7 Ave Invermere
- Columbia Cycle and Ski, 375 Laurier Ave Invermere
- Inside Edge Sports, 905 7 Ave Invermere
- Far Out Adventure Hub, Outdoor Gear Rentals, 7514 Main Street Radium

Guides
- Playwest Hiking Guides, Invermere https://playwest.ca
- East Kootenay Mountain Guides, Invermere www.ekmountainguides.com

Useful Websites for hiking in the Columbia Valley
- Columbia Valley Hikes Facebook Group
- Golden Scrambles covers many peaks in the Columbia Valley though the information is a few years old: https://www.goldenscrambles.ca/
- Golden area trails https://goldenhikes.ca/
- Greenways trail alliance https://www.greenways.ca/
- Nipika Mountain Resort https://nipika.com/
- Panorama webcam https://www.panoramaresort.com/panorama-today/mountain-webcams/
- Columbia Valley Hut Society https://cvhsinfo.org/
- Kootenay Park Trail Report https://www.pc.gc.ca/en/pn-np/bc/kootenay/activ/randonnee-hike/etat-sentiers-trail-conditions
- BC Parks trail reports for Bugaboo, Purcell Wilderness, Top of the World, and Height of the Rockies https://bcparks.ca/explore/
- Summit Trailmakers Society http://www.summittrailmakers.ca/

Mountain Weather
https://spotwx.com/
https://www.panoramaresort.com/panorama-today/daily-snow-report/
(scroll past the daily snow report for the year round alpine weather forecast)
https://www.avalanche.ca/weather/forecast (available year round)

Safety
Wildsafe https://wildsafebc.com/
Adventuresmart https://www.adventuresmart.ca/

ABOUT THE AUTHORS

Stefanie Mclellan has roamed around these mountains for over 15 years. She enjoys reading maps and old guidebooks and is always planning the next adventure. Her favorite mountain partners are her husband Cam and her border collie Henry.

When she is not out in the mountains, whether hiking, skiing, biking or climbing, she works as a physician in Invermere.

Corinna Strauss lives in Invermere and works in the environmental field, doing a number of activities - from wildlife education to five needle pine conservation. She has lived in the Rocky Mountains and the Columbia Valley for nearly two decades. Corinna enjoys being outside in the mountains: exploring, running, climbing, hiking, skiing and biking. Corinna loves exploring with her dog Ila Bean and an incredible community of other inspiring explorers and adventurers.

INDEX